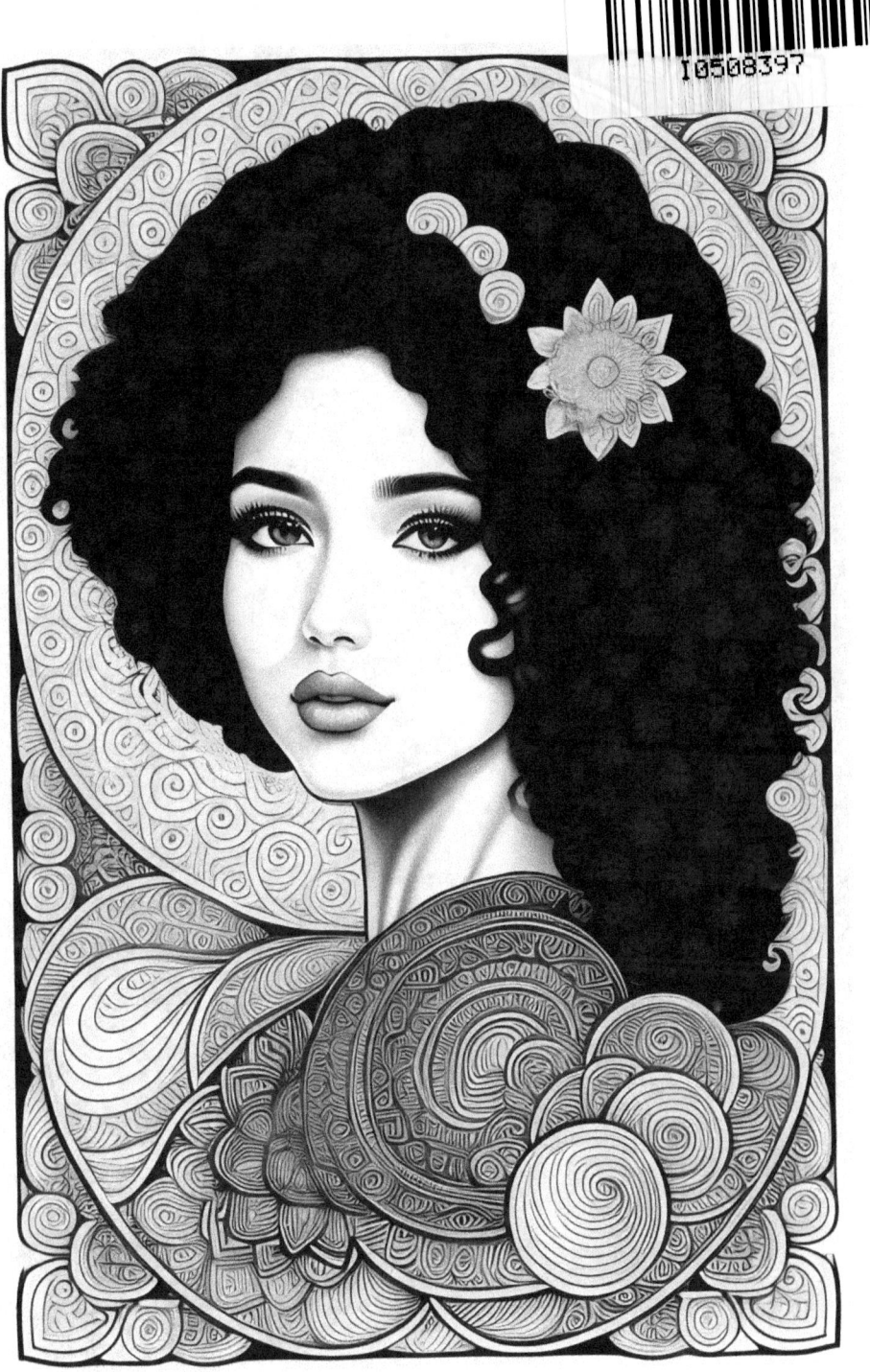

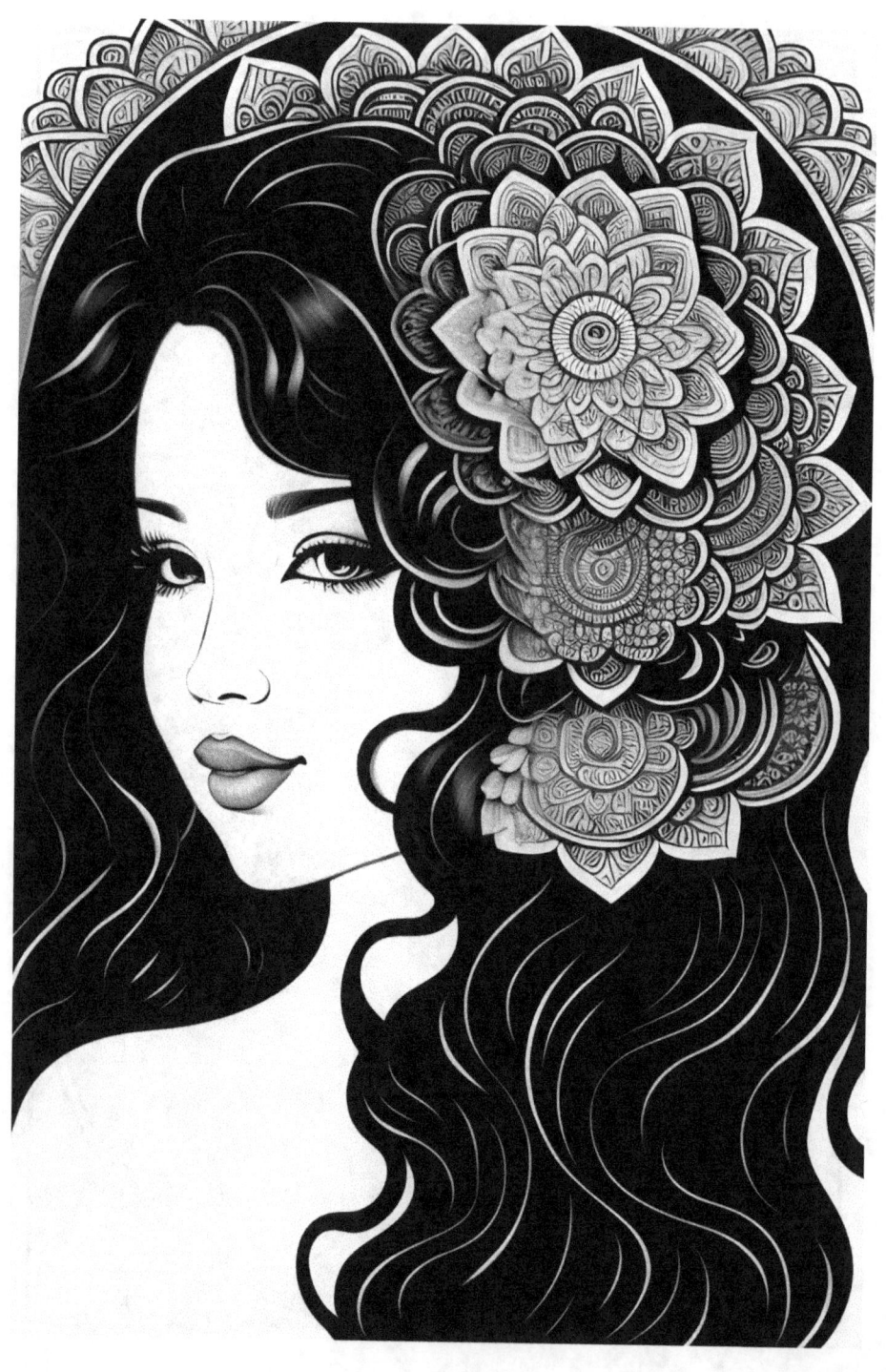

Awesome Coloring Book for Adults

introduction

Welcome to the "Awesome Coloring Book for Adults"! This book is more than just coloring pages – it's an invitation to explore your creative side, immerse yourself in an oasis of tranquility, and discover the joy of artistic expression.

With its intricate and captivating illustrations, carefully designed for adults, you'll be transported to a world of vibrant colors and endless possibilities. Free your mind from everyday worries, let the stress fade away, and indulge in hours of relaxation as you fill each page with your own choices of colors and unique combinations.

Whether you're an experienced artist seeking a creative break or a beginner looking for a new way to express yourself, this book is a sanctuary where your imagination can flourish.

Get ready for a visually stunning journey where each brushstroke is an opportunity for discovery and self-discovery. So, grab your colored pencils, take a deep breath, and embark on this exciting adult coloring adventure.

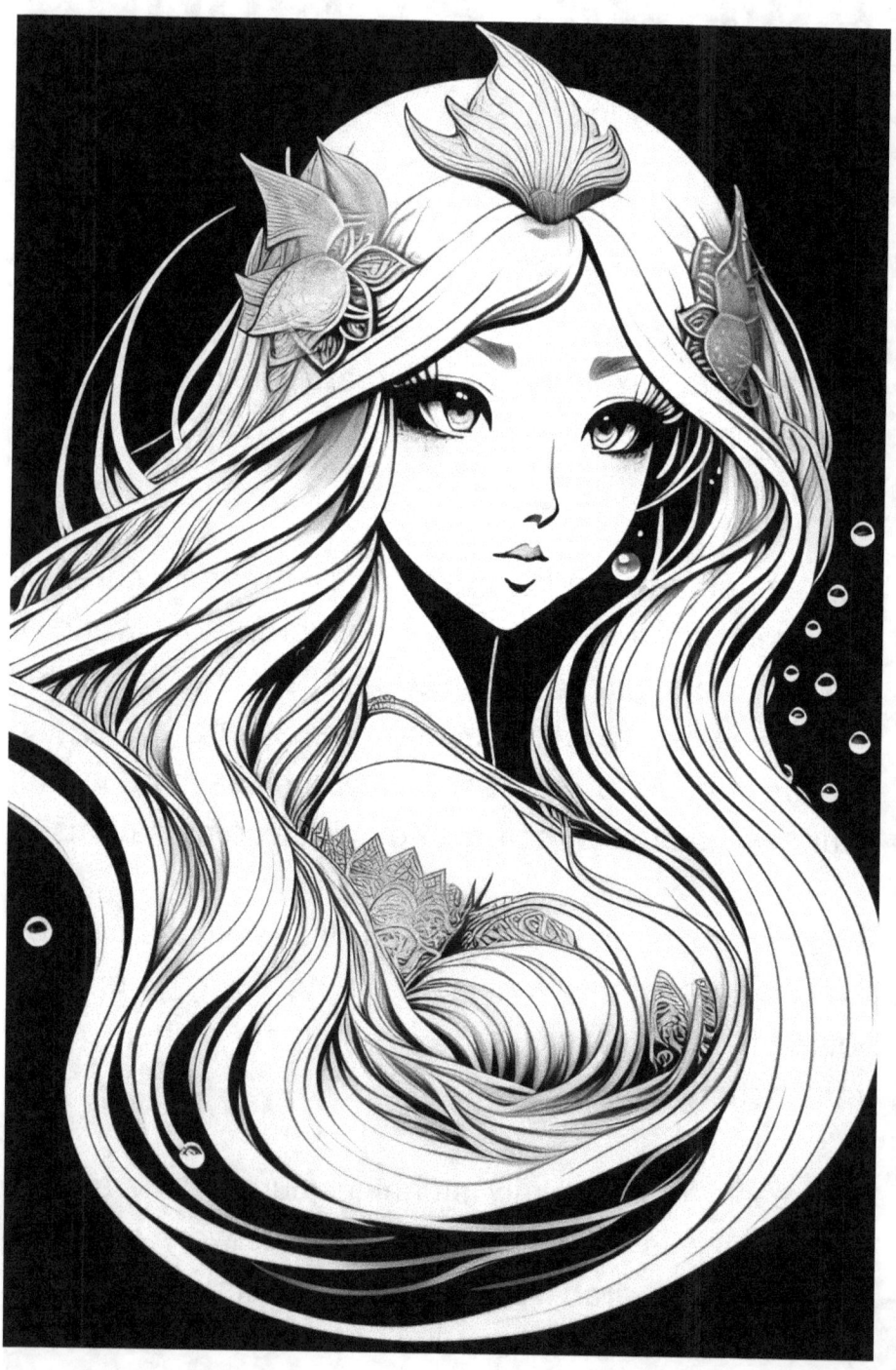

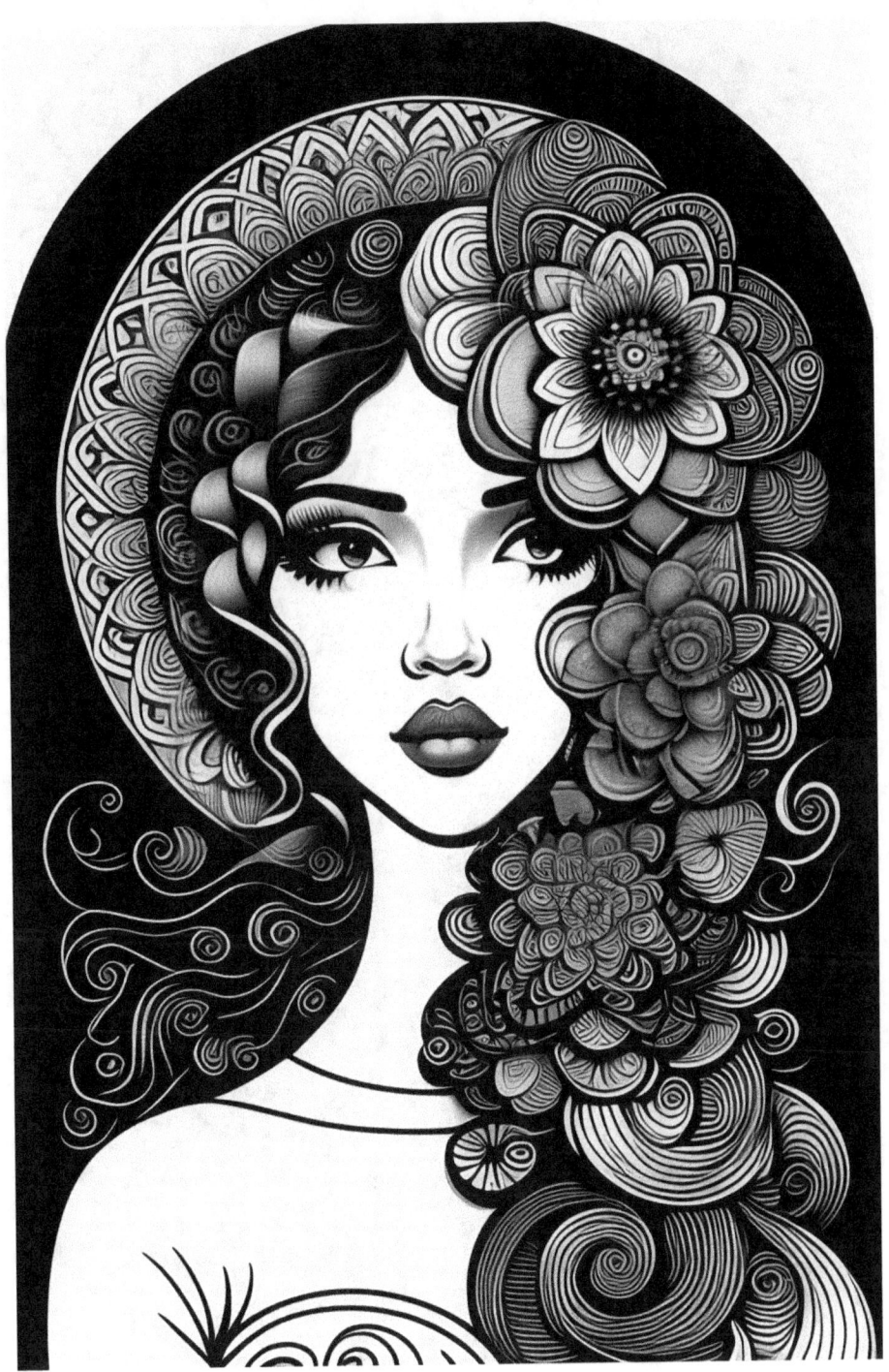

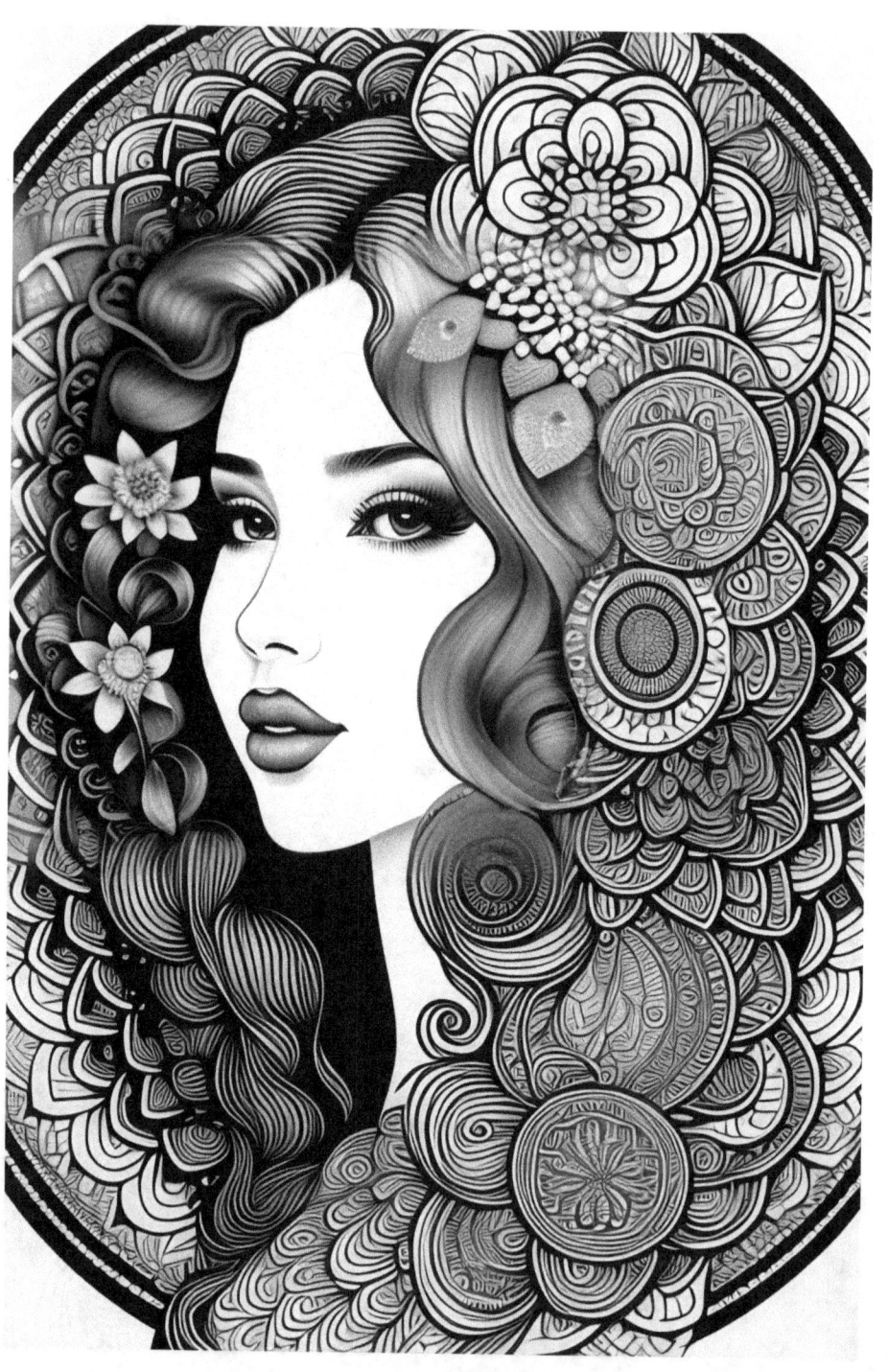

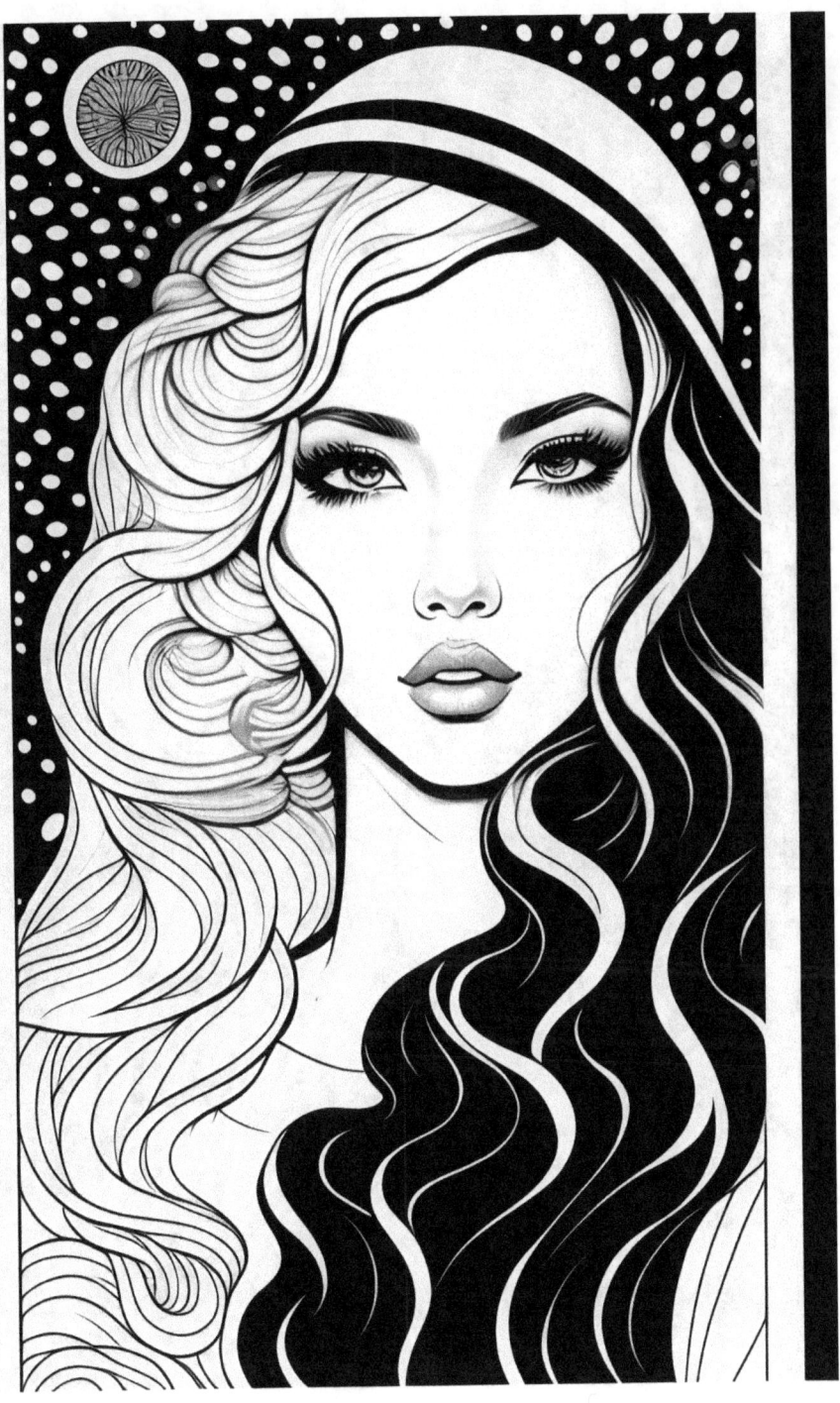

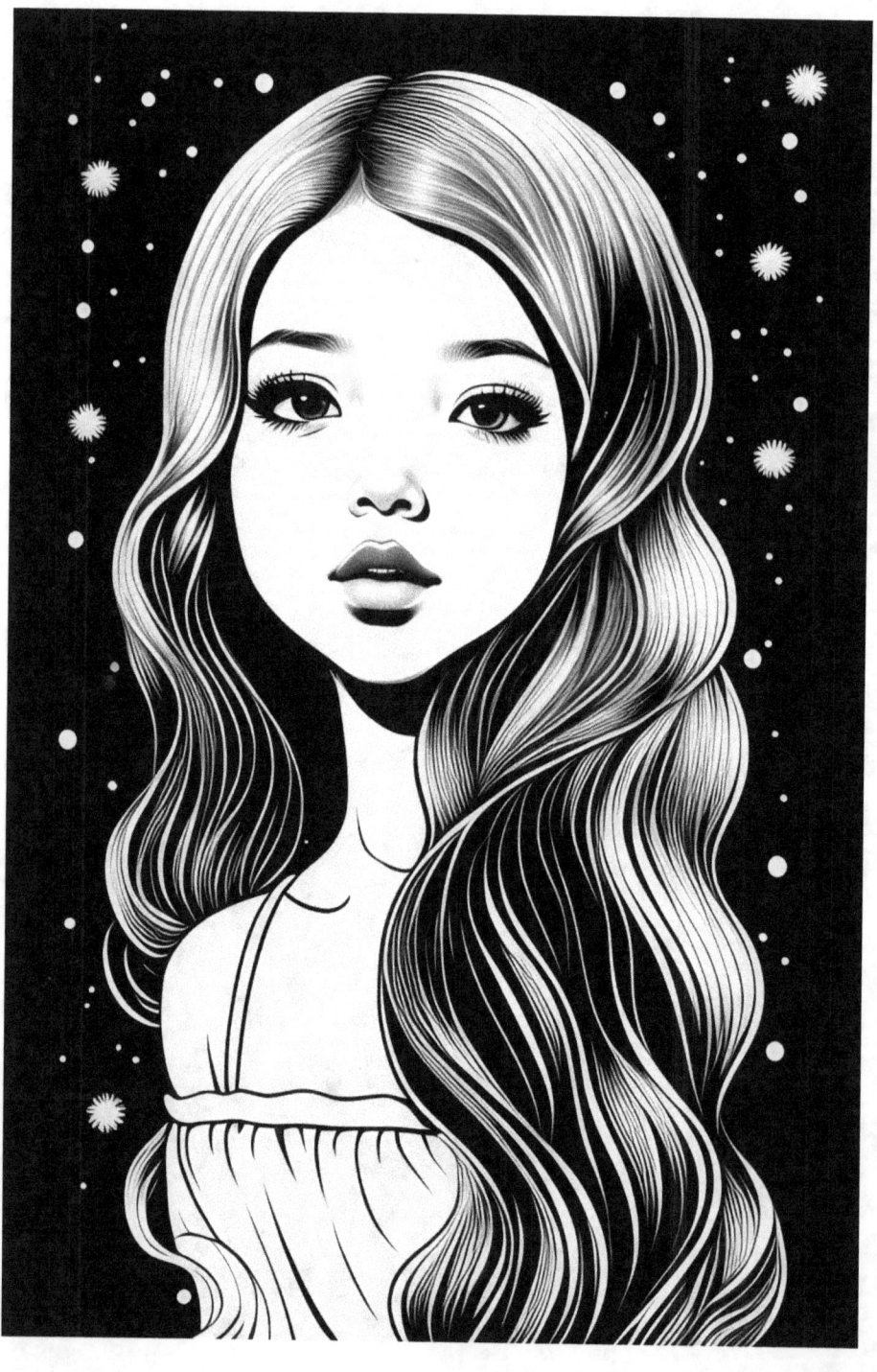

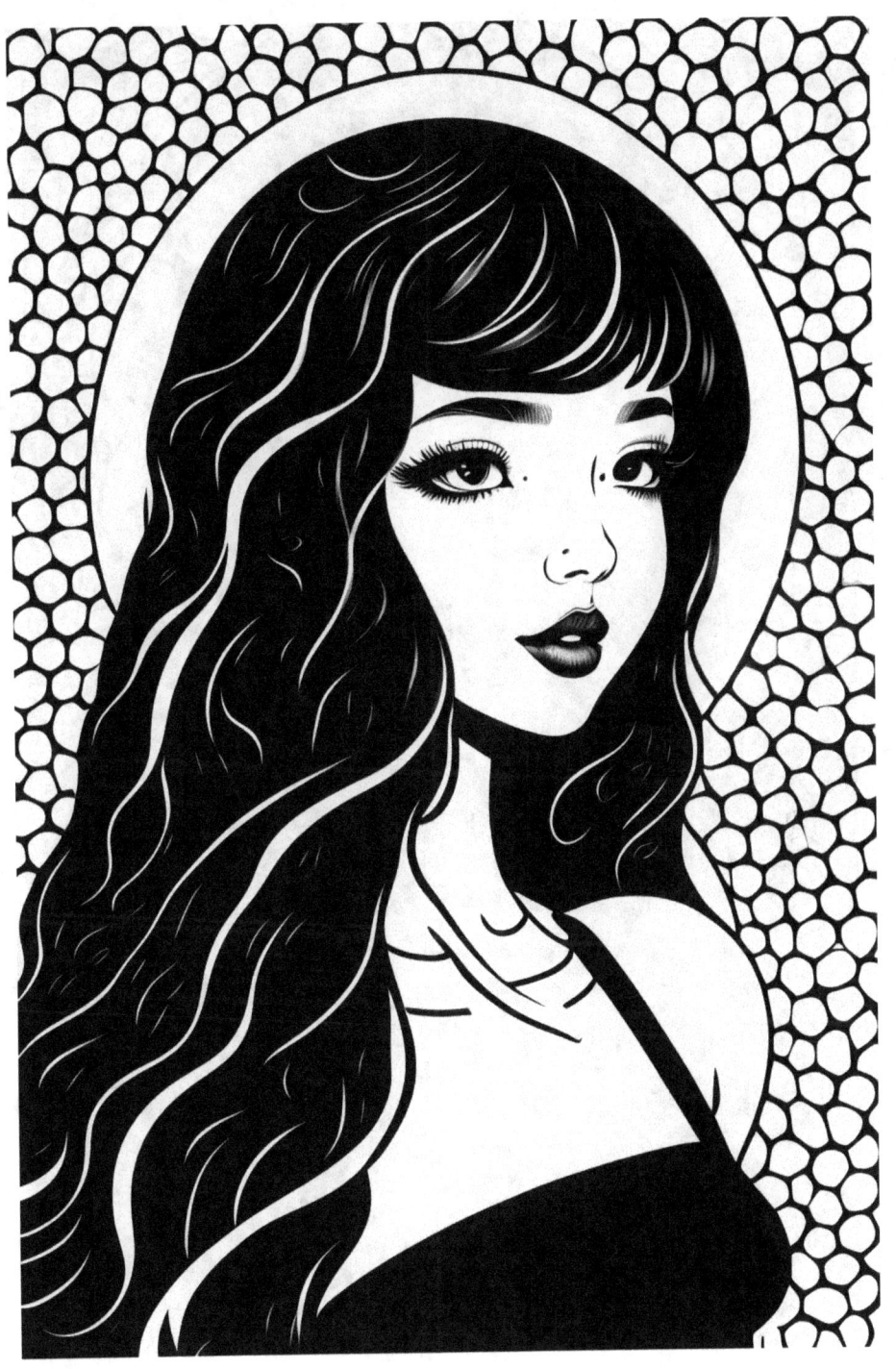

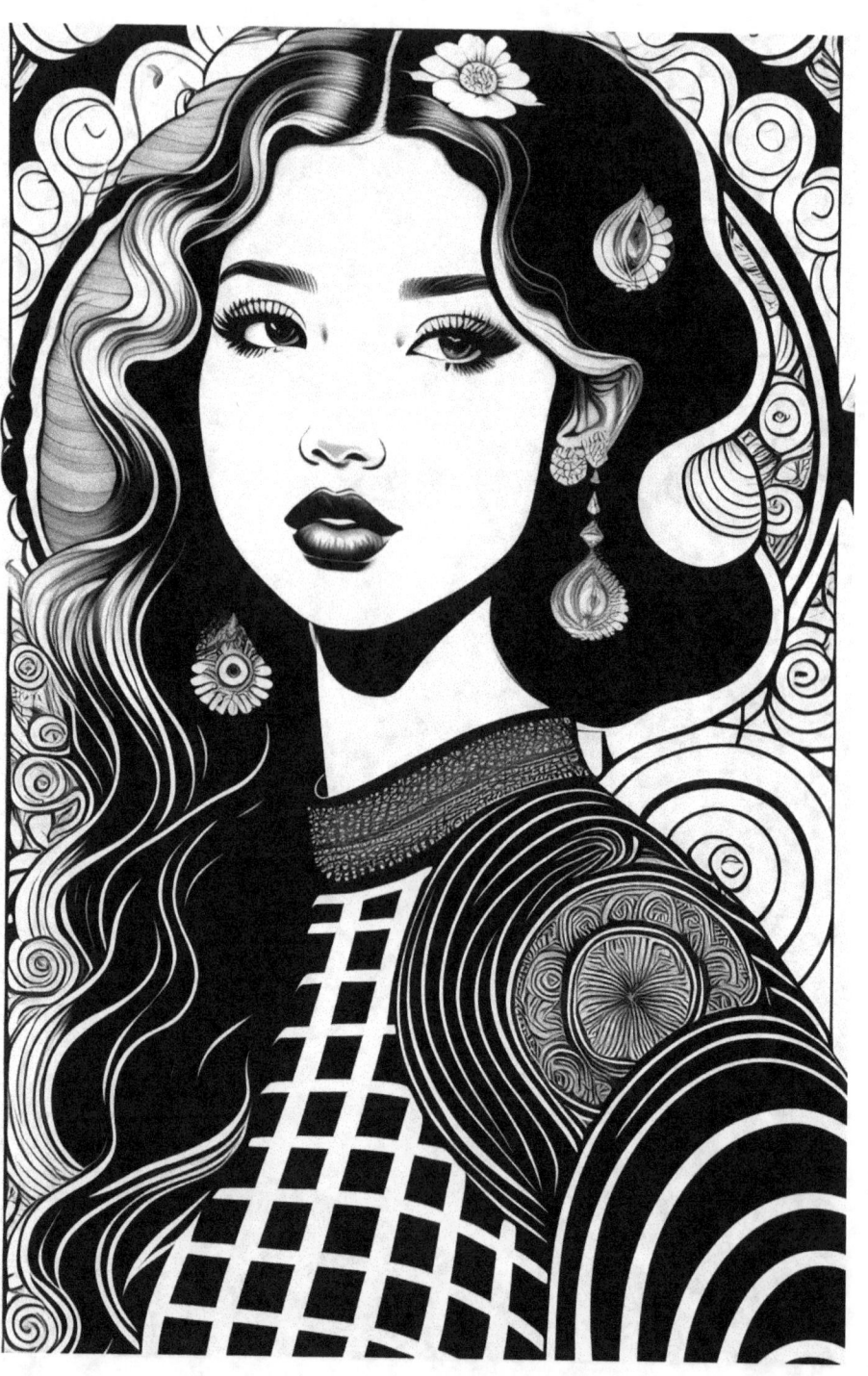

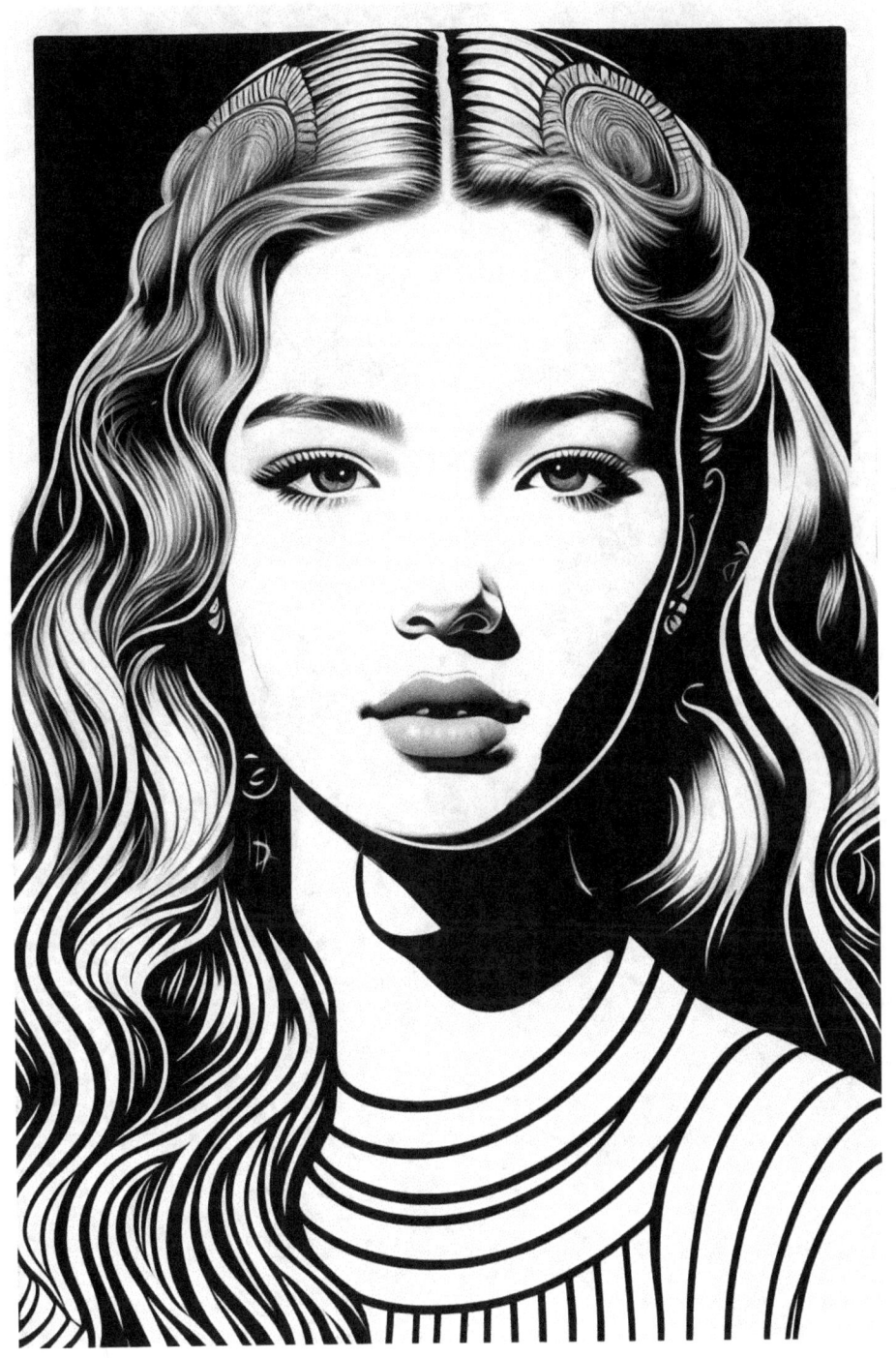

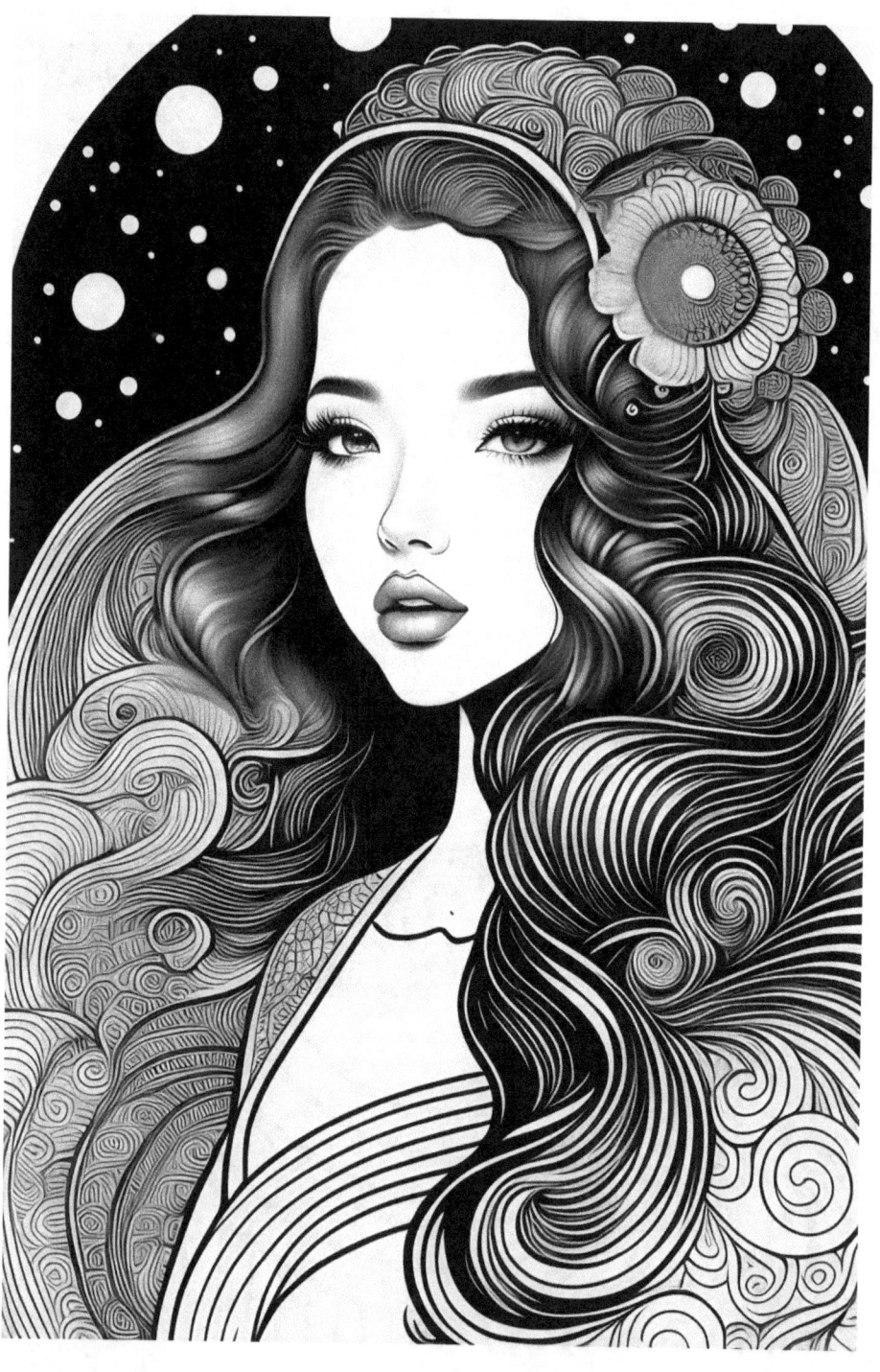

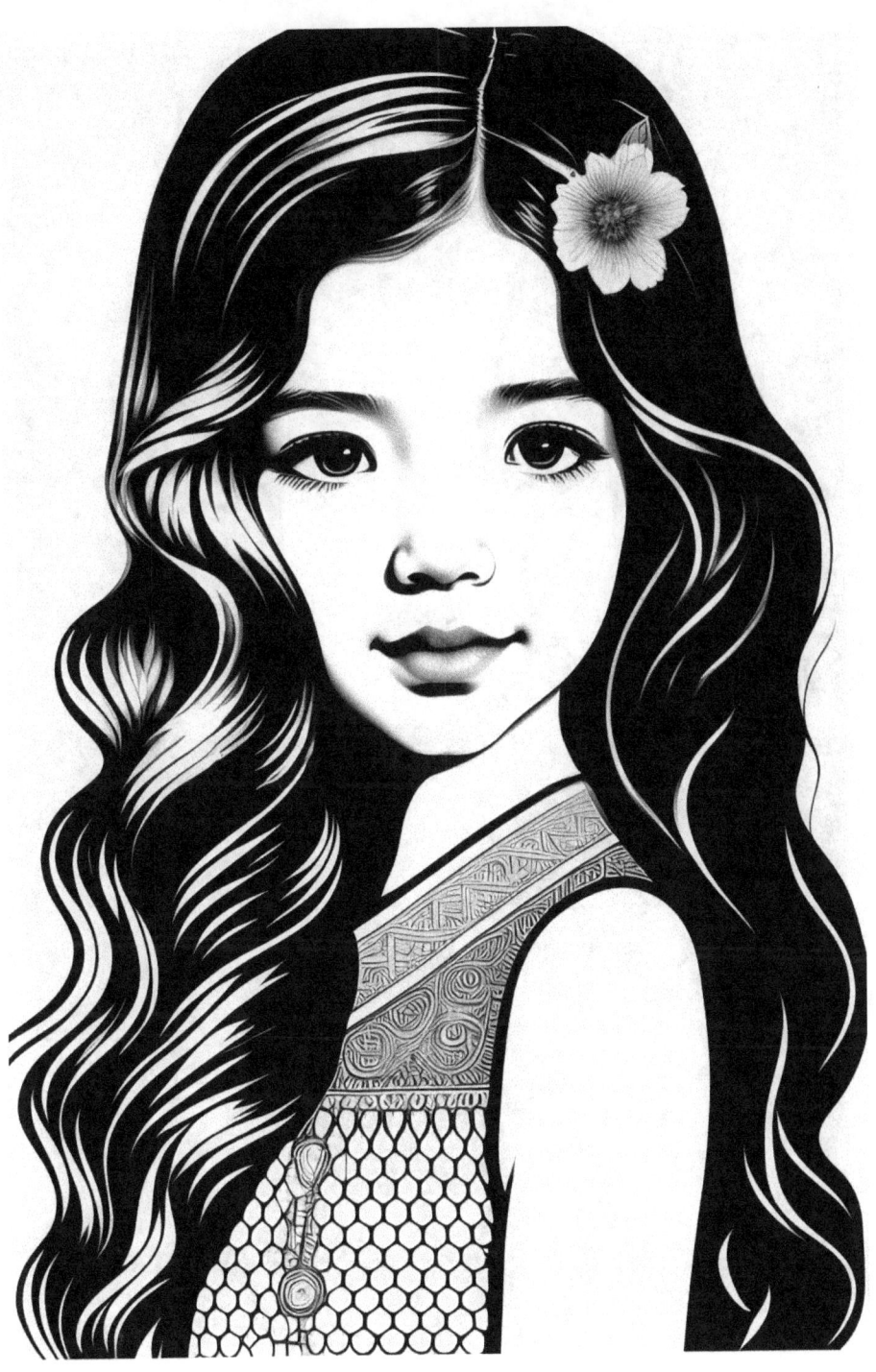

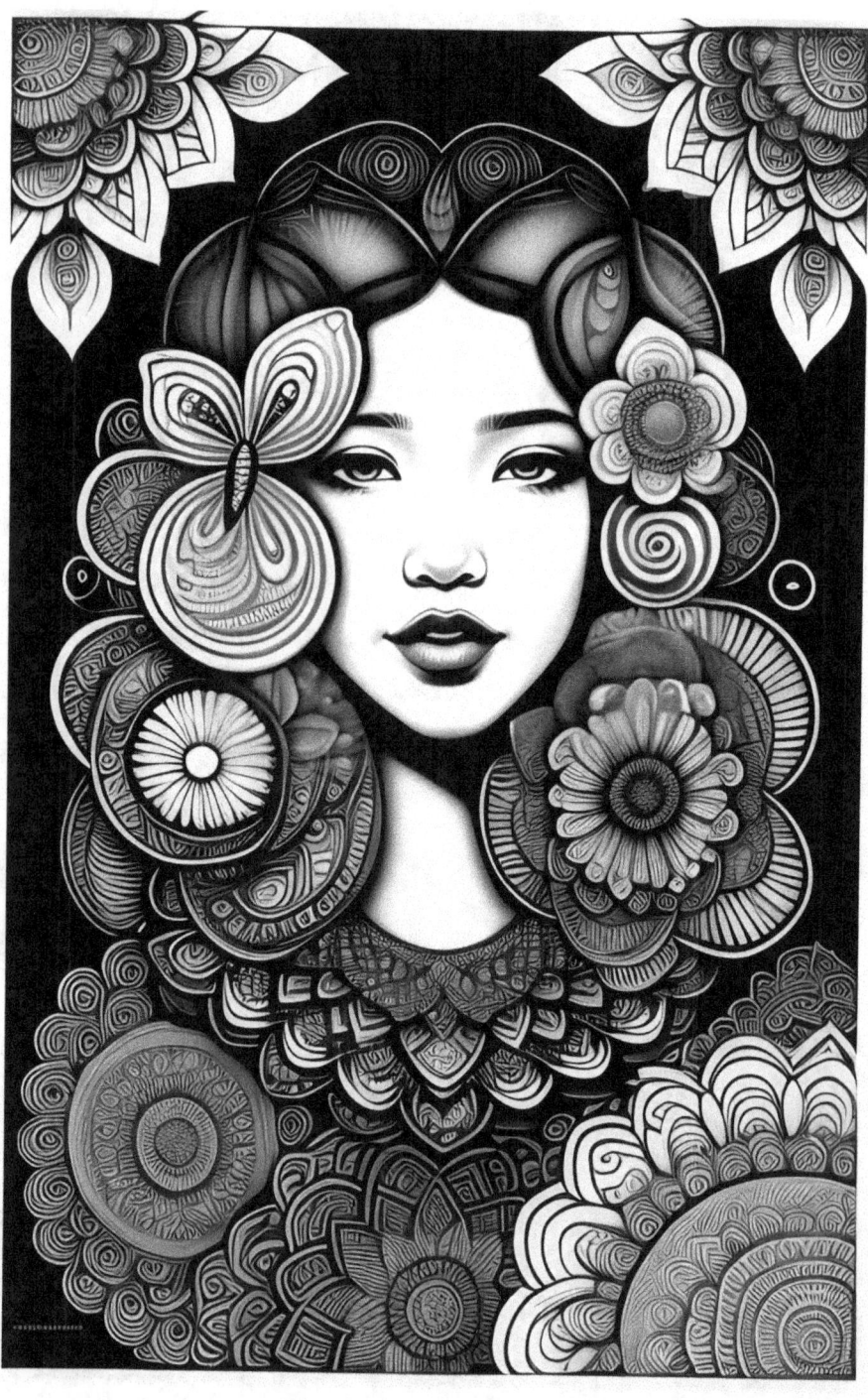

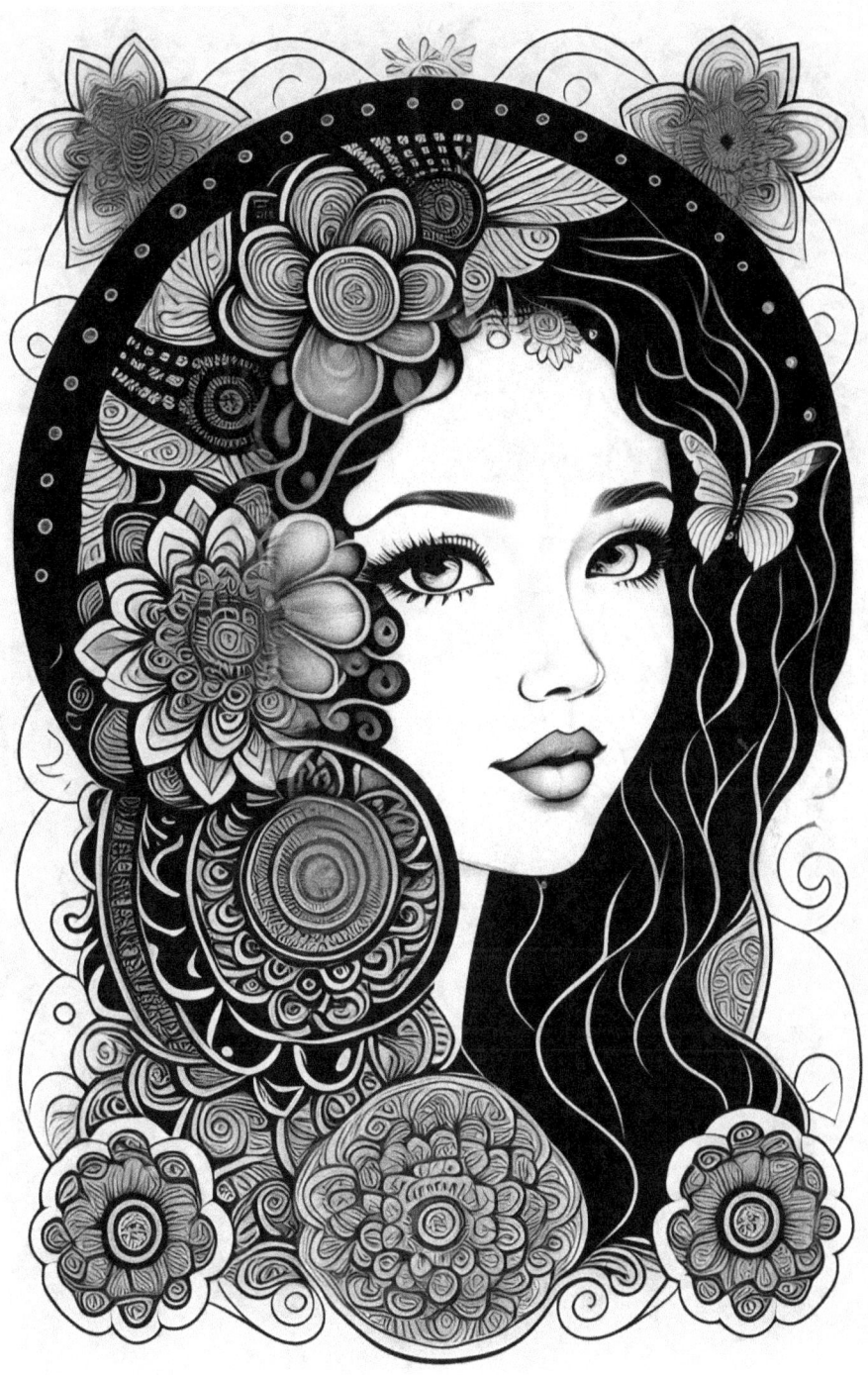

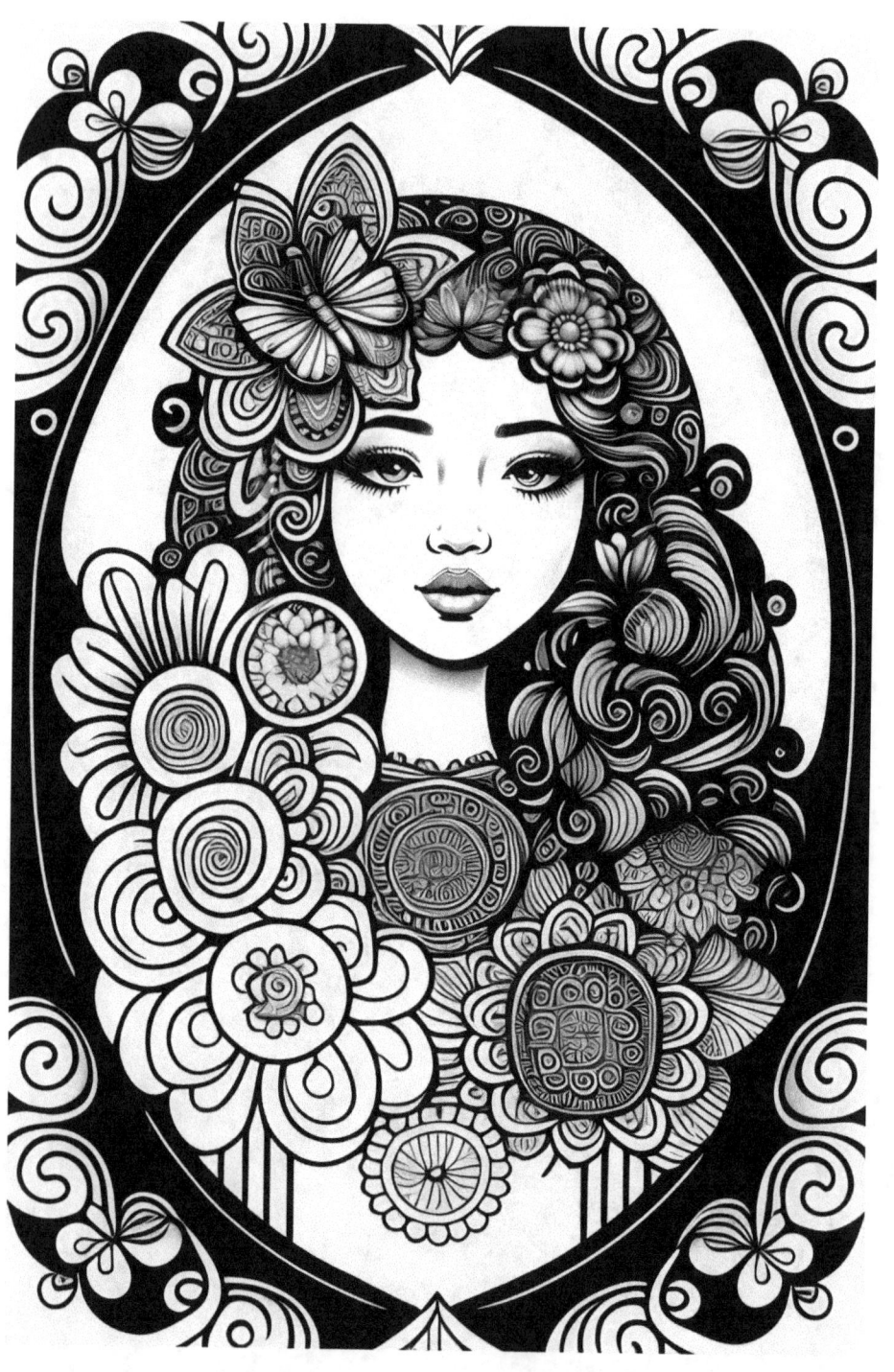

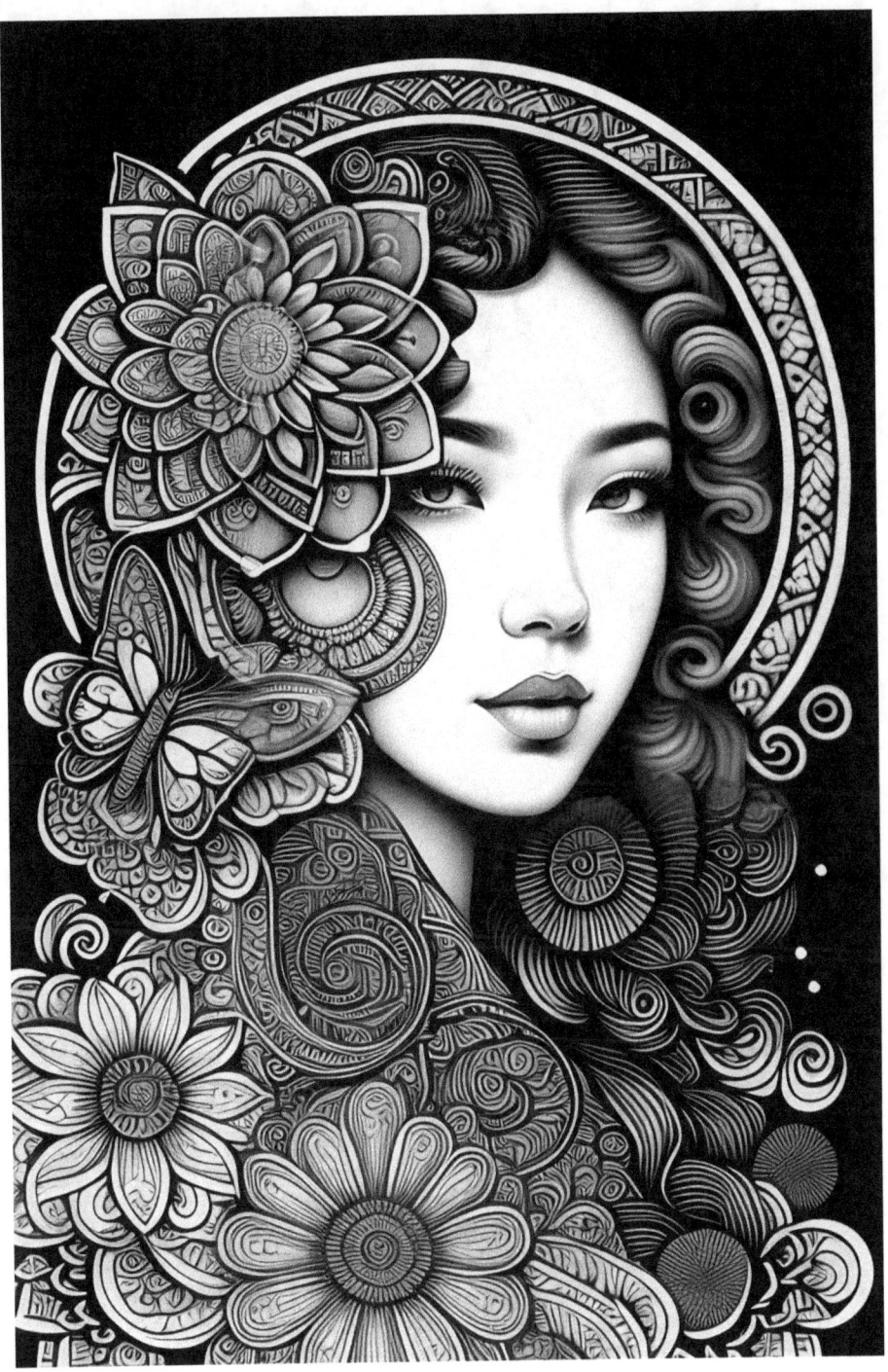

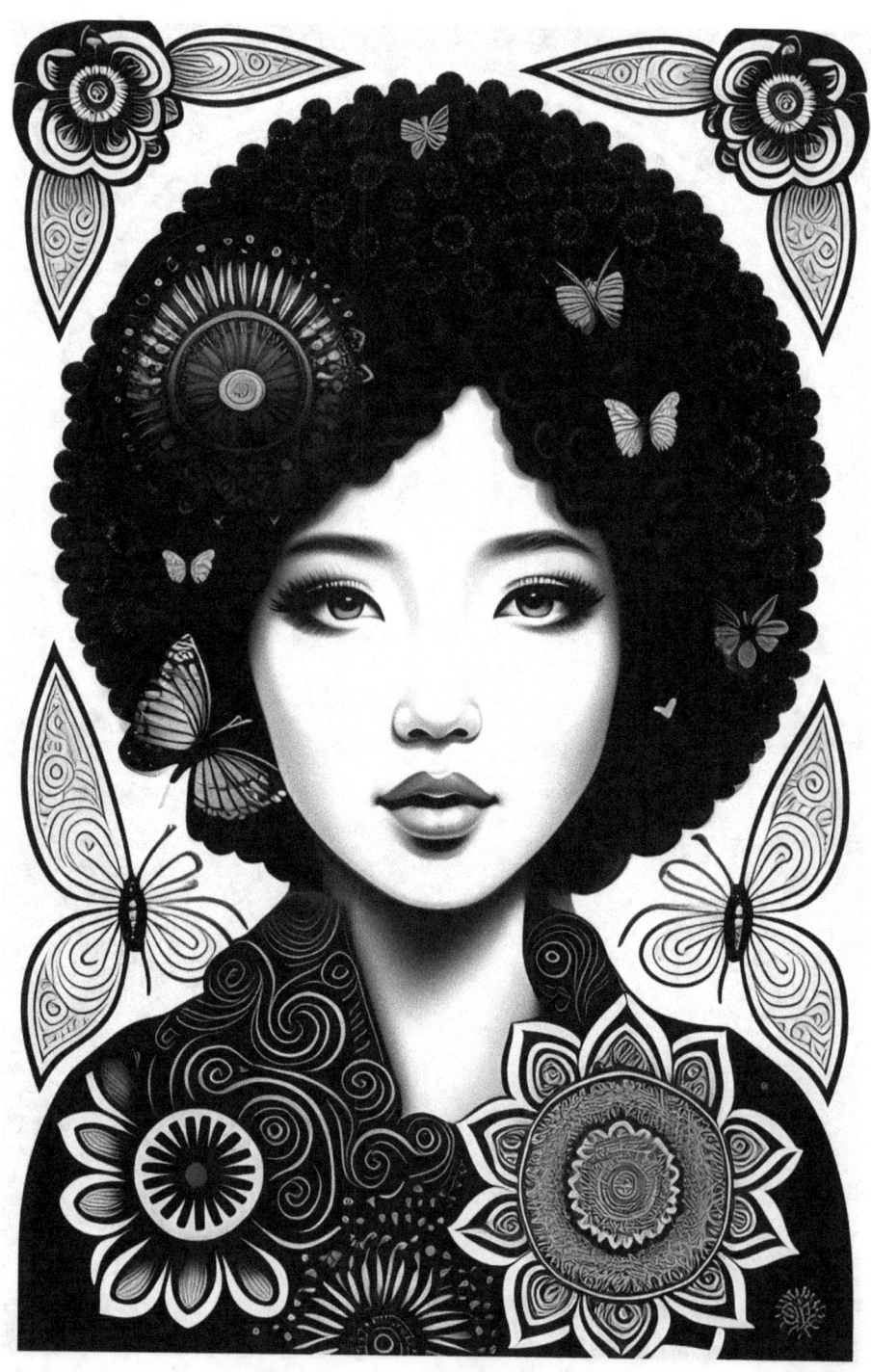

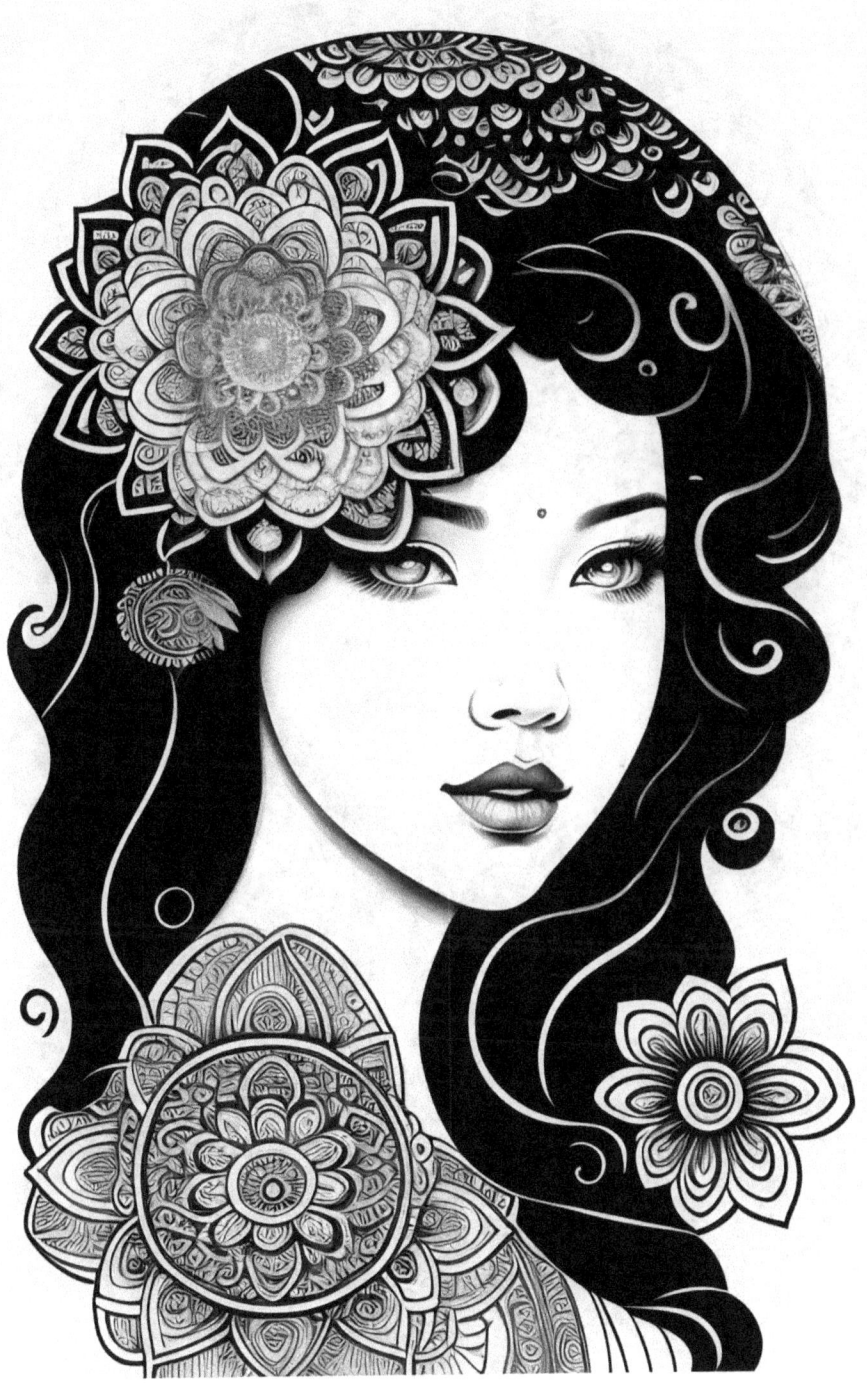

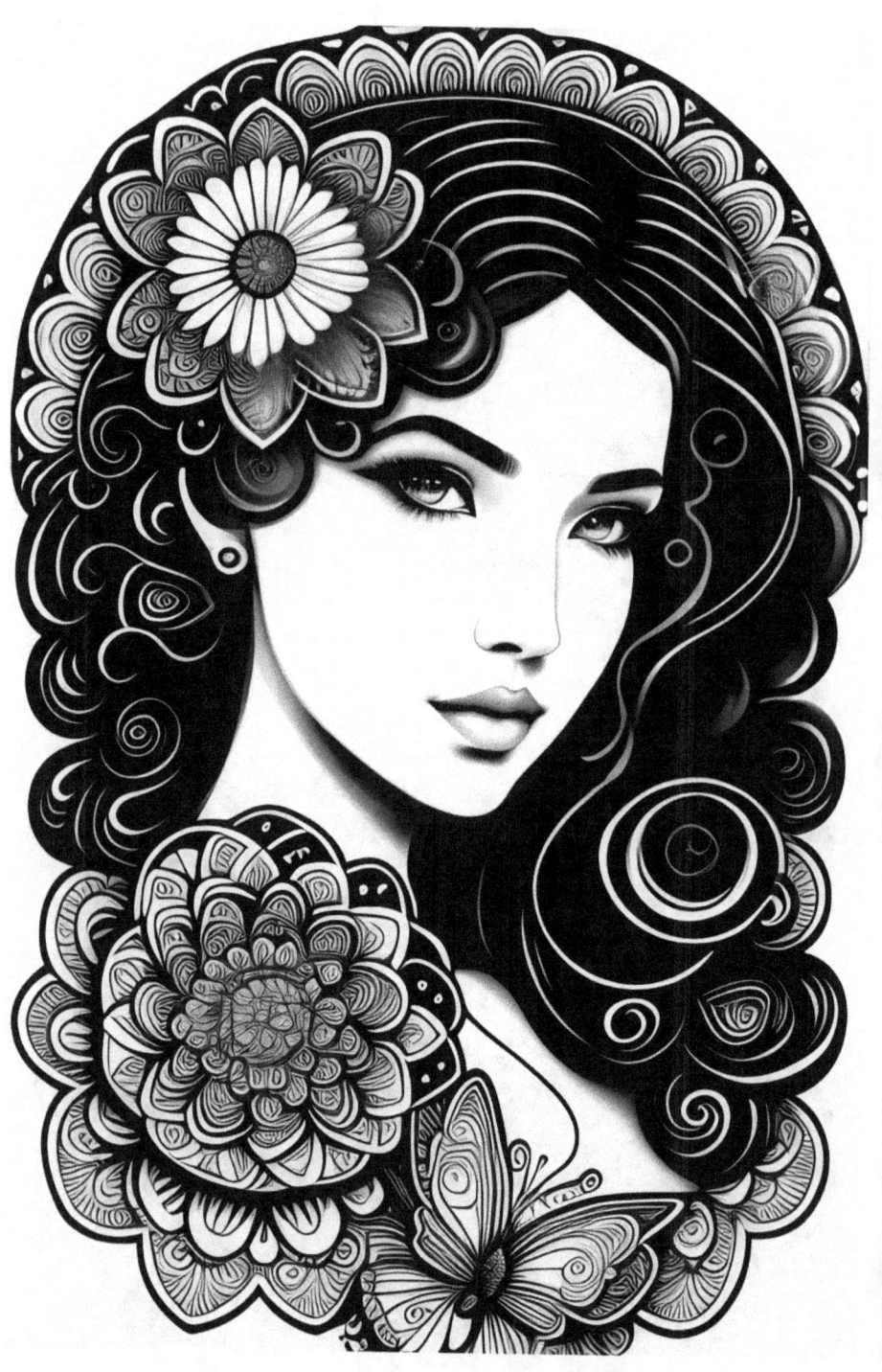

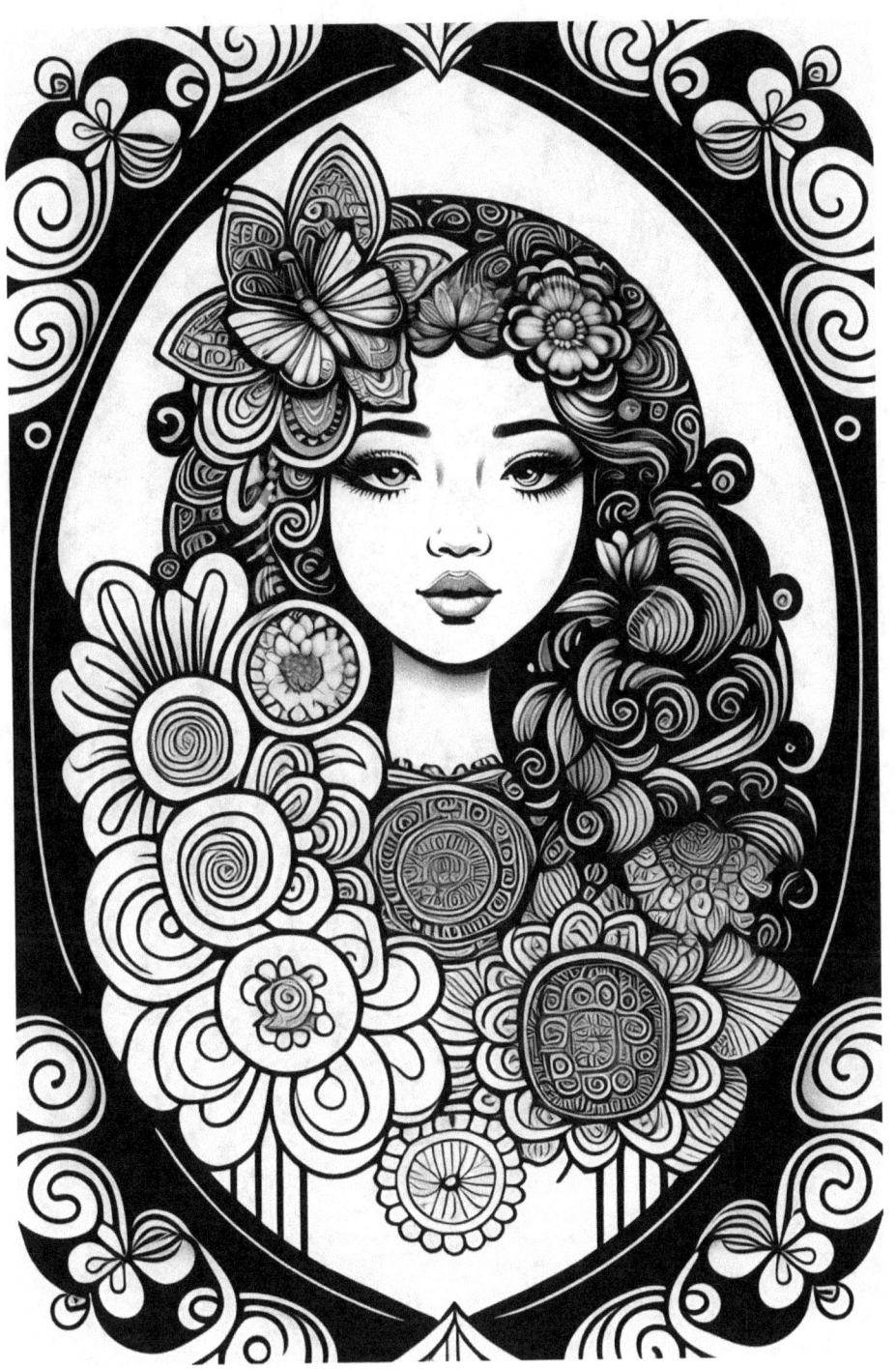

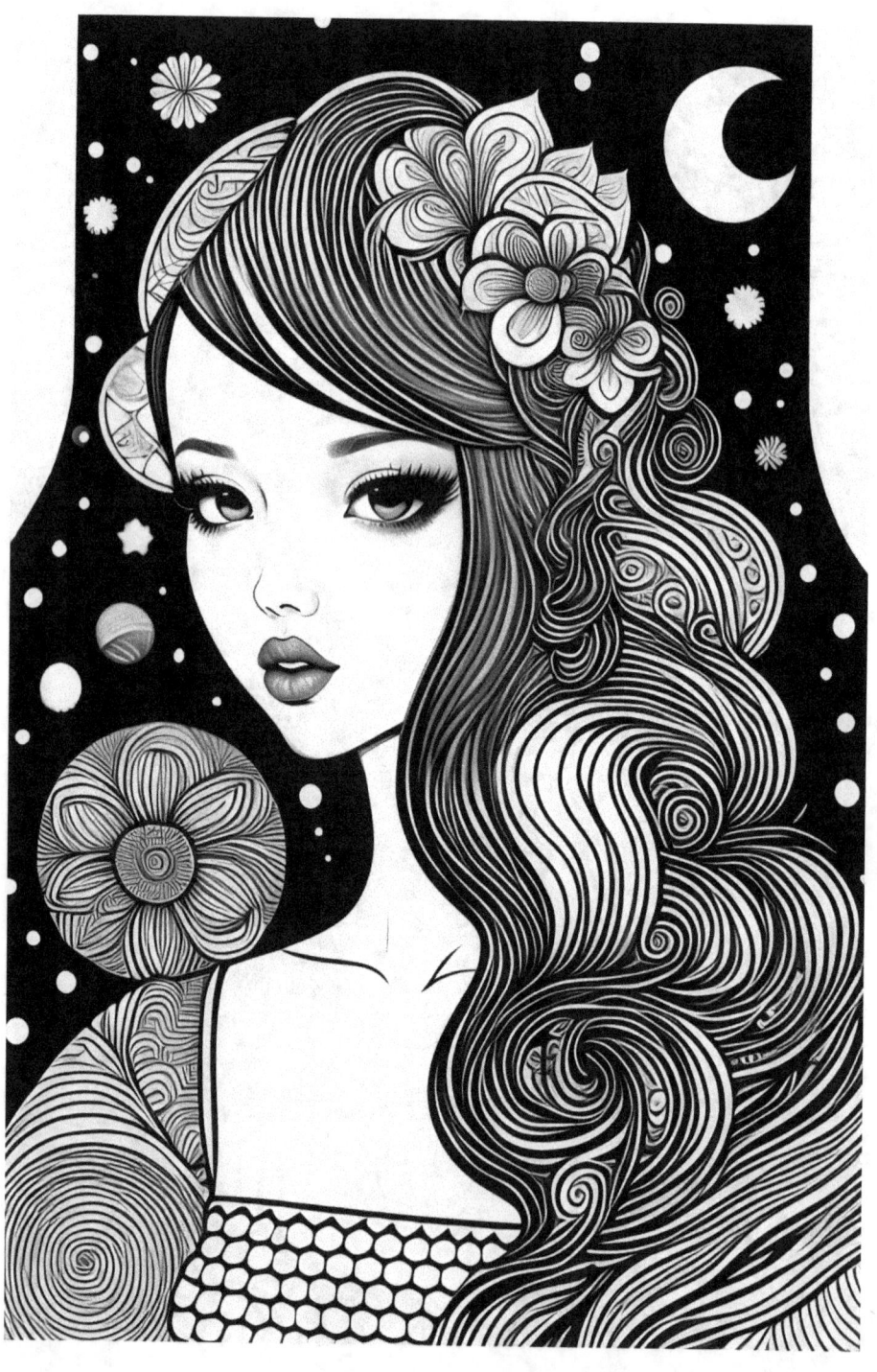

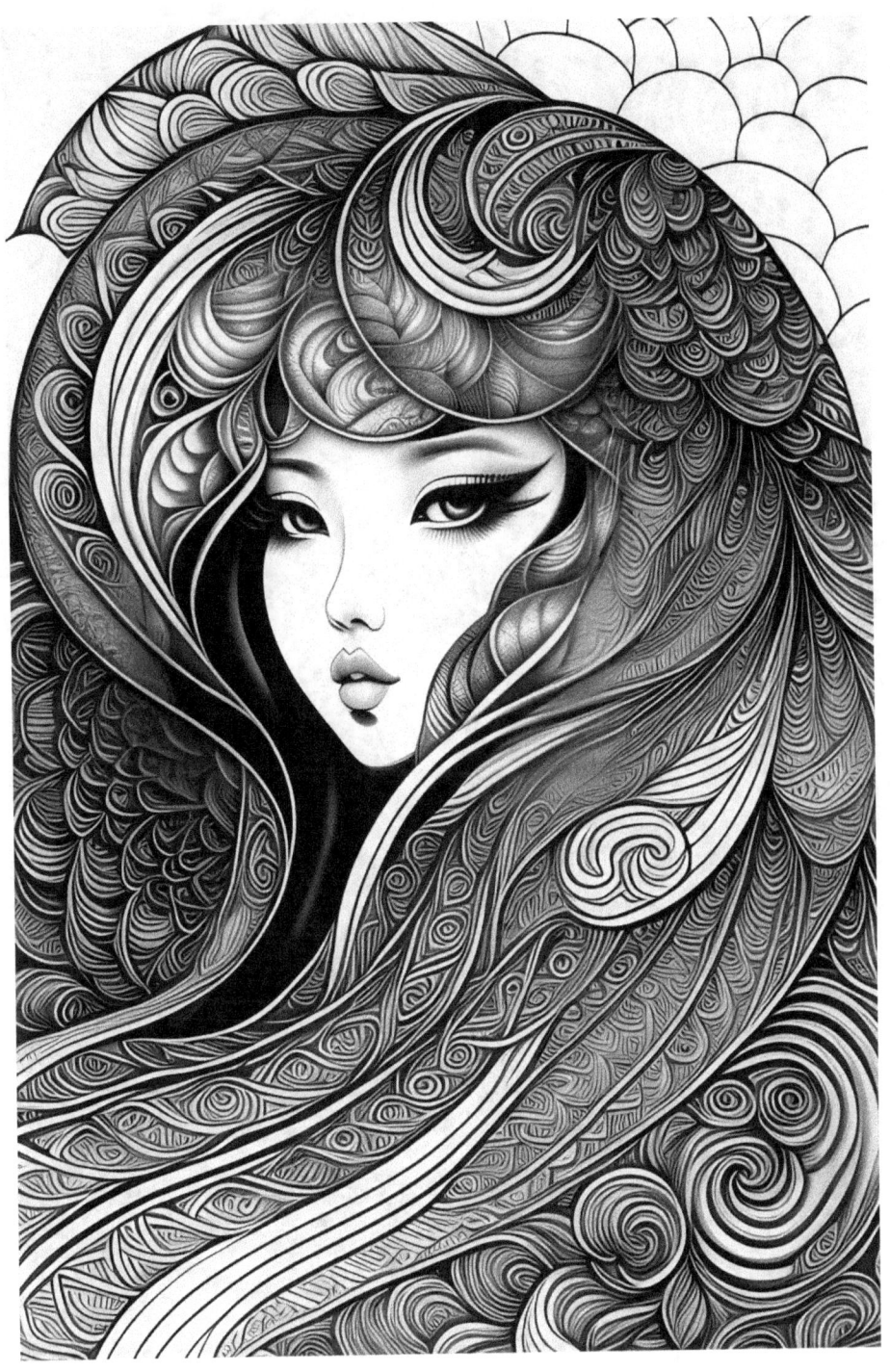

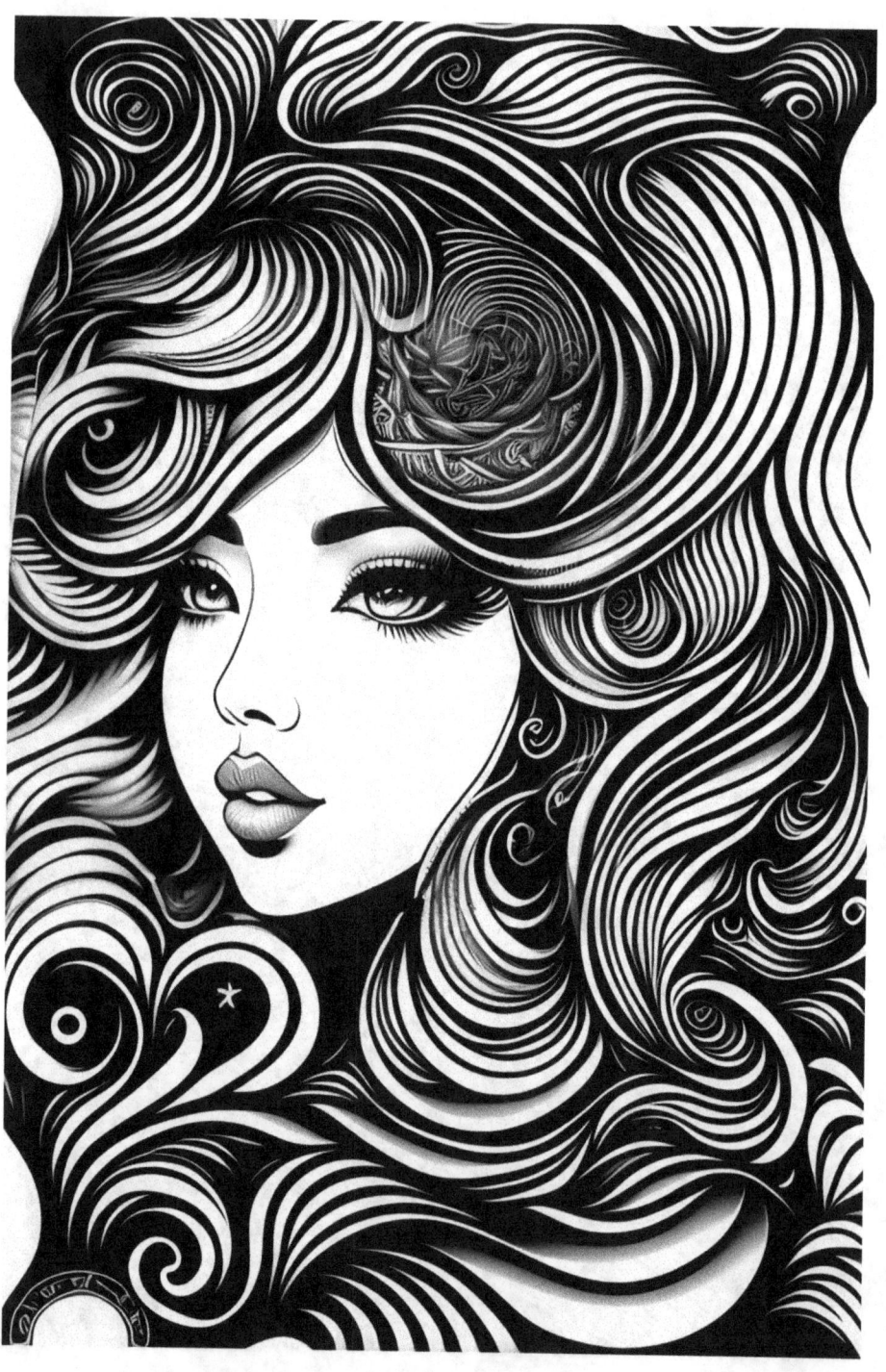

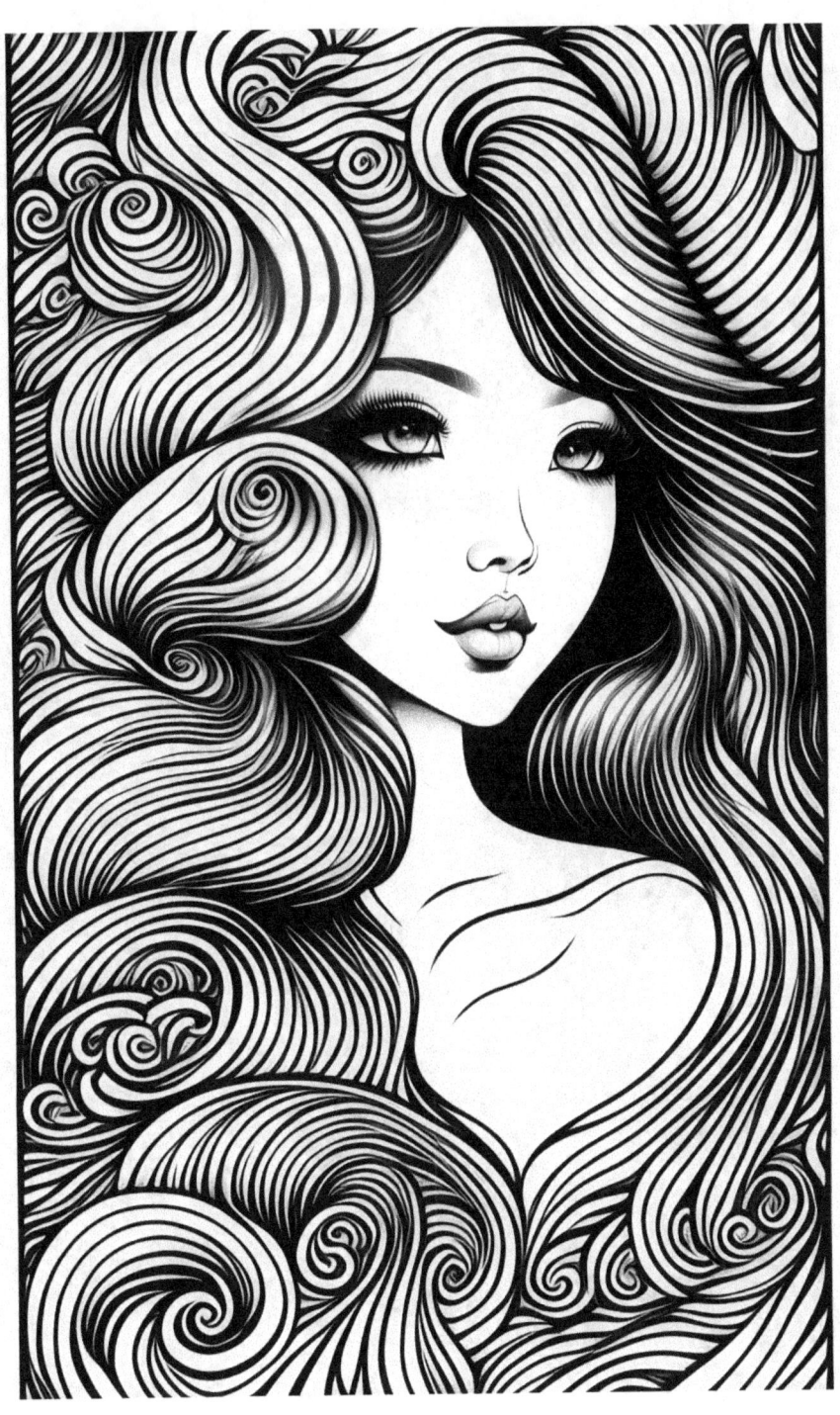

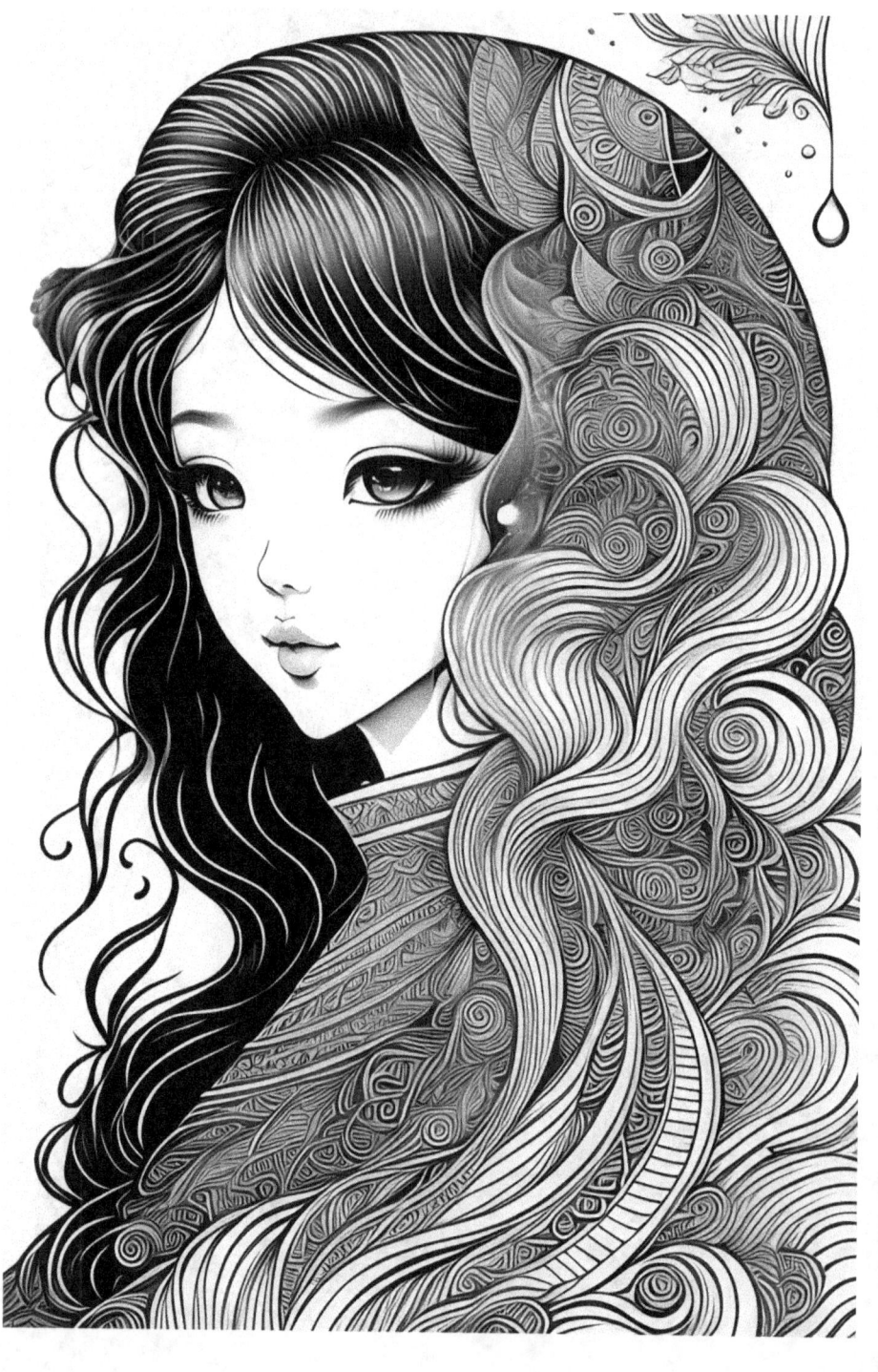

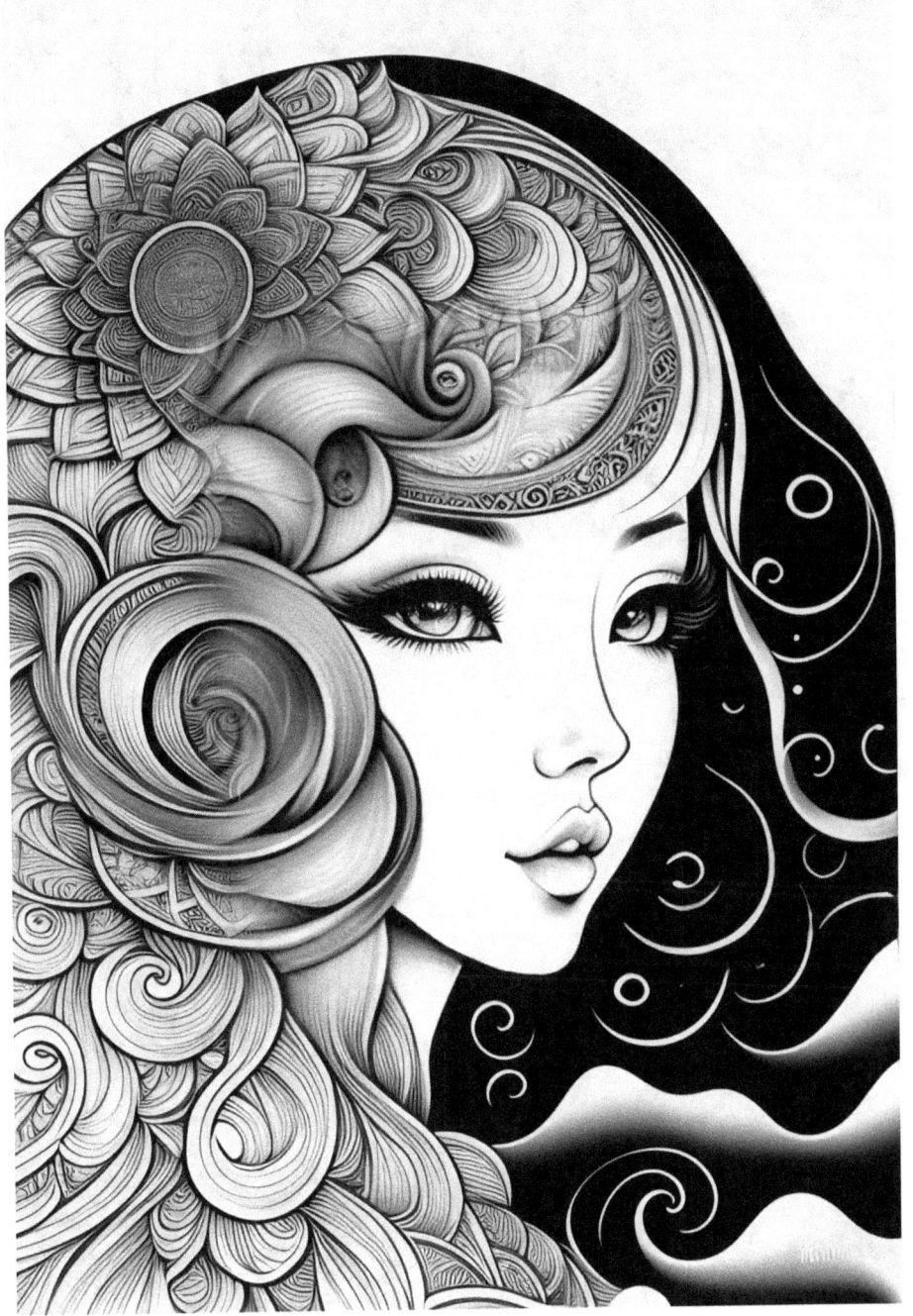

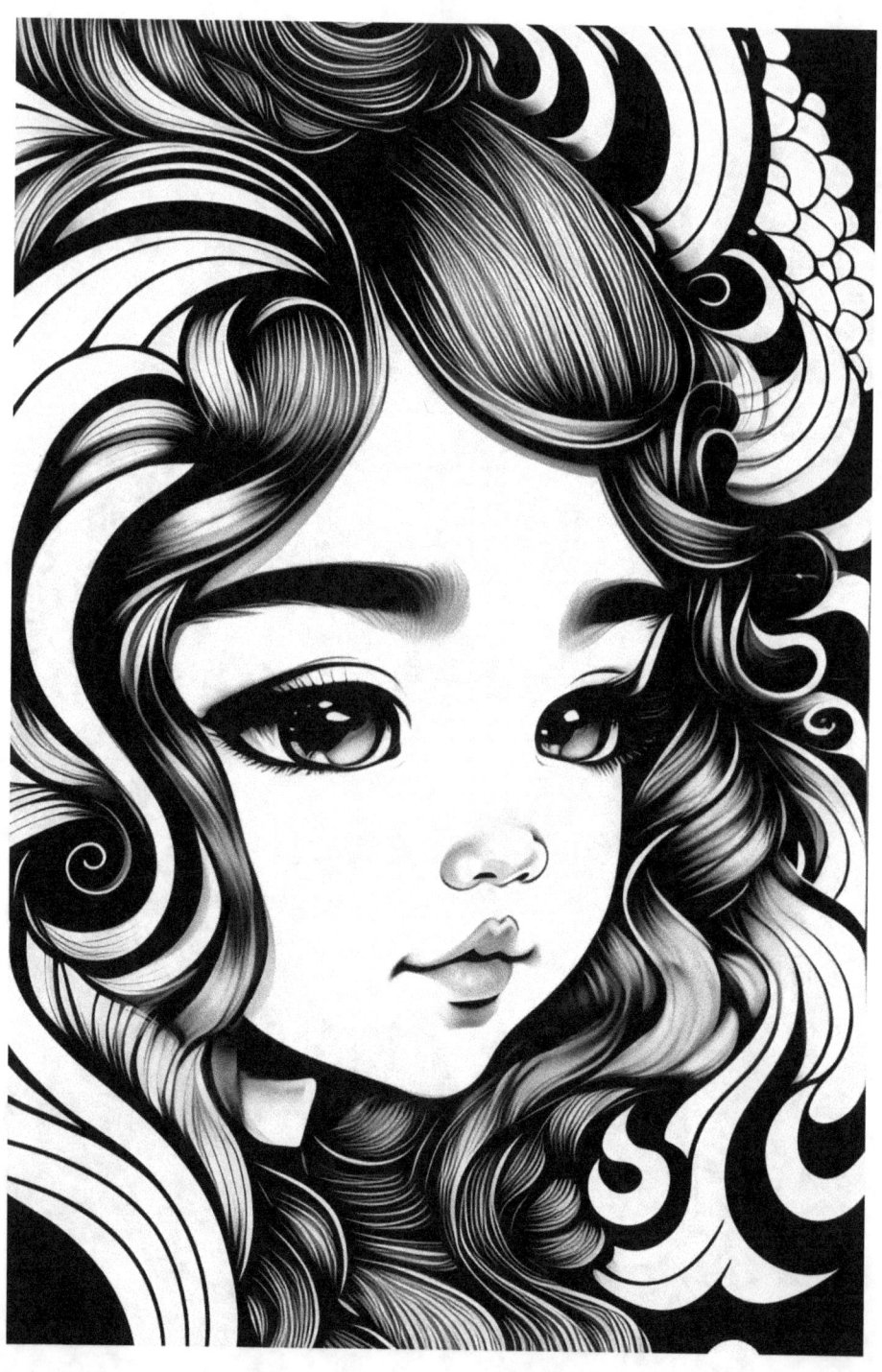

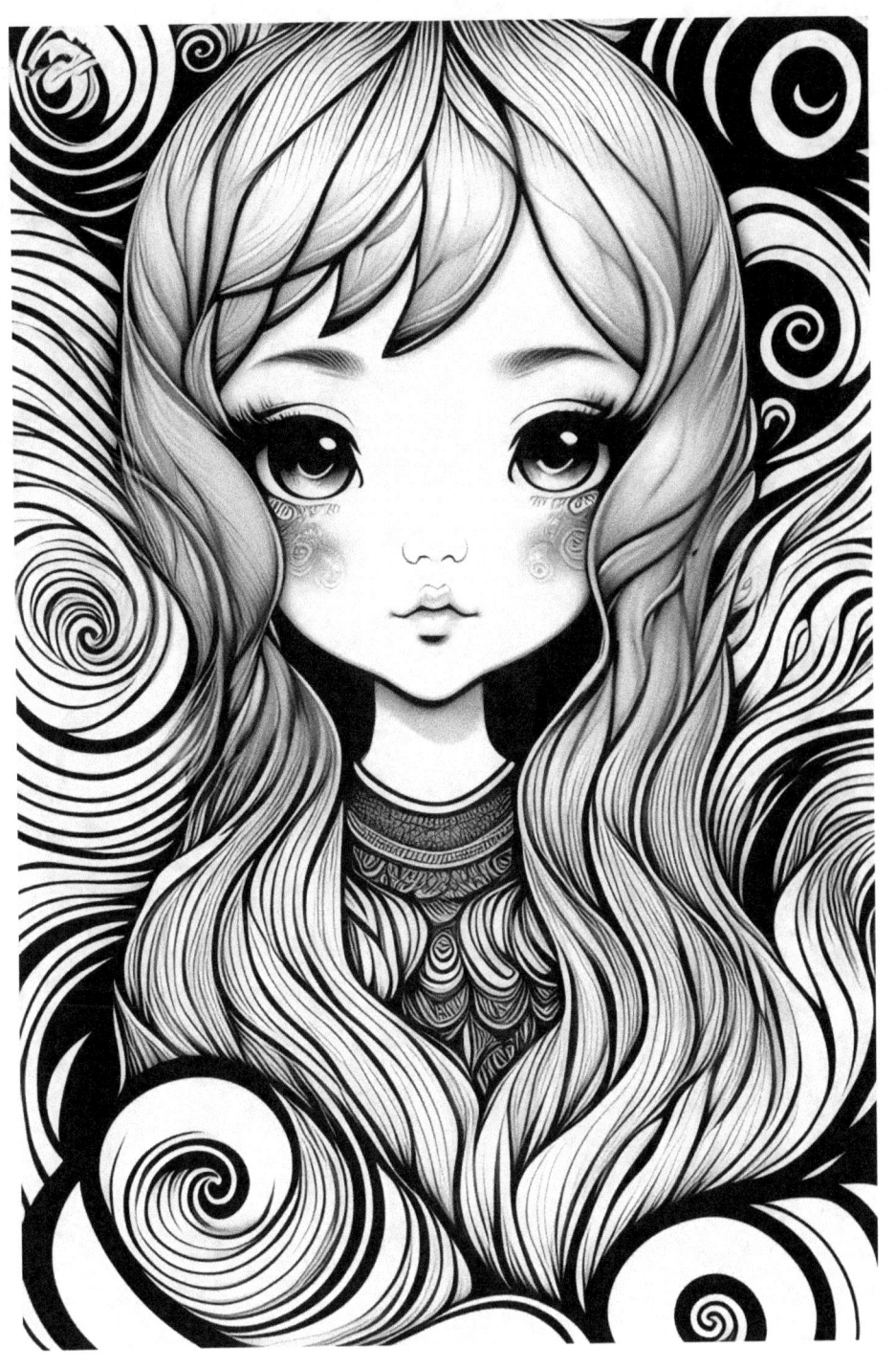

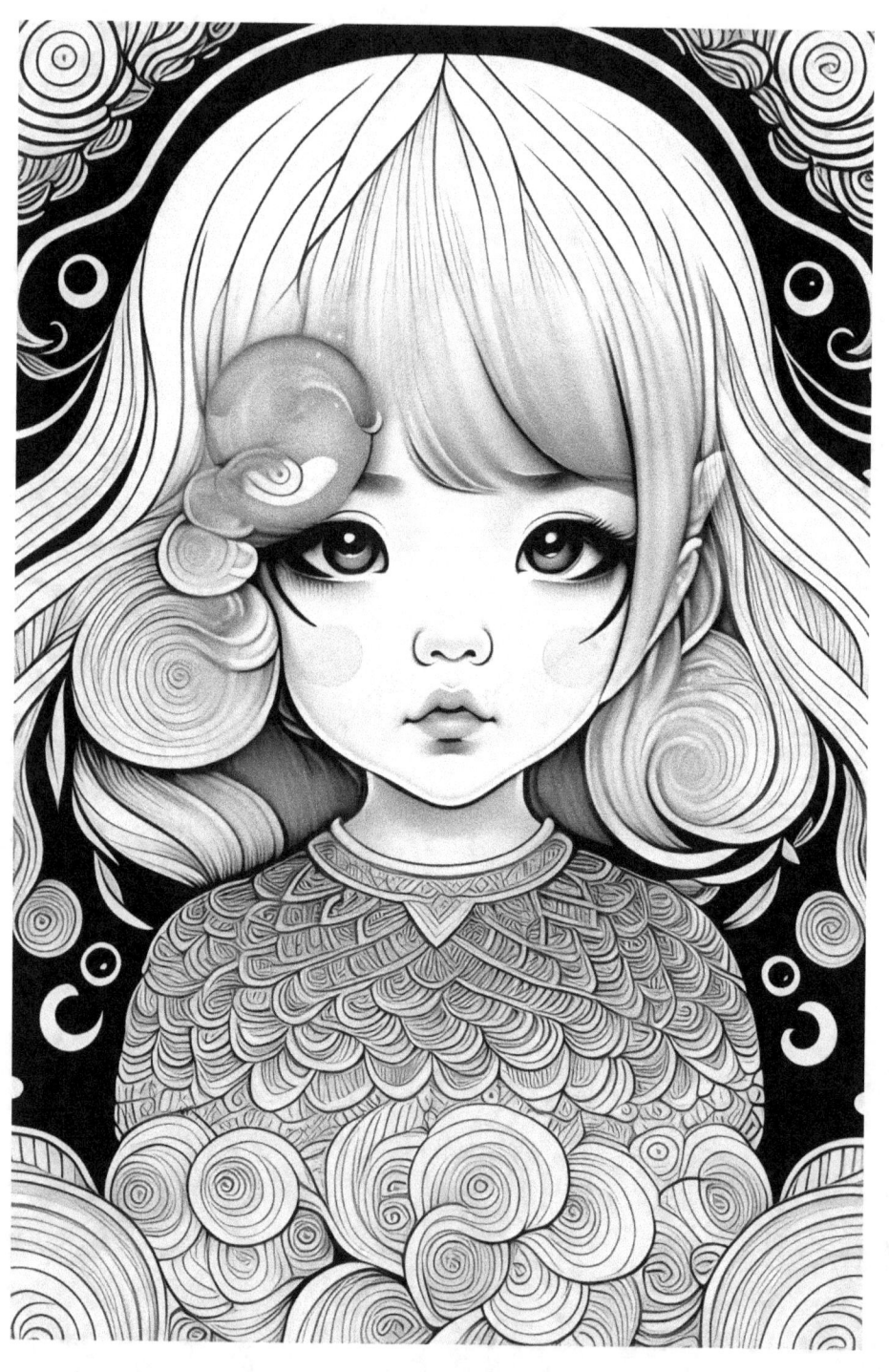

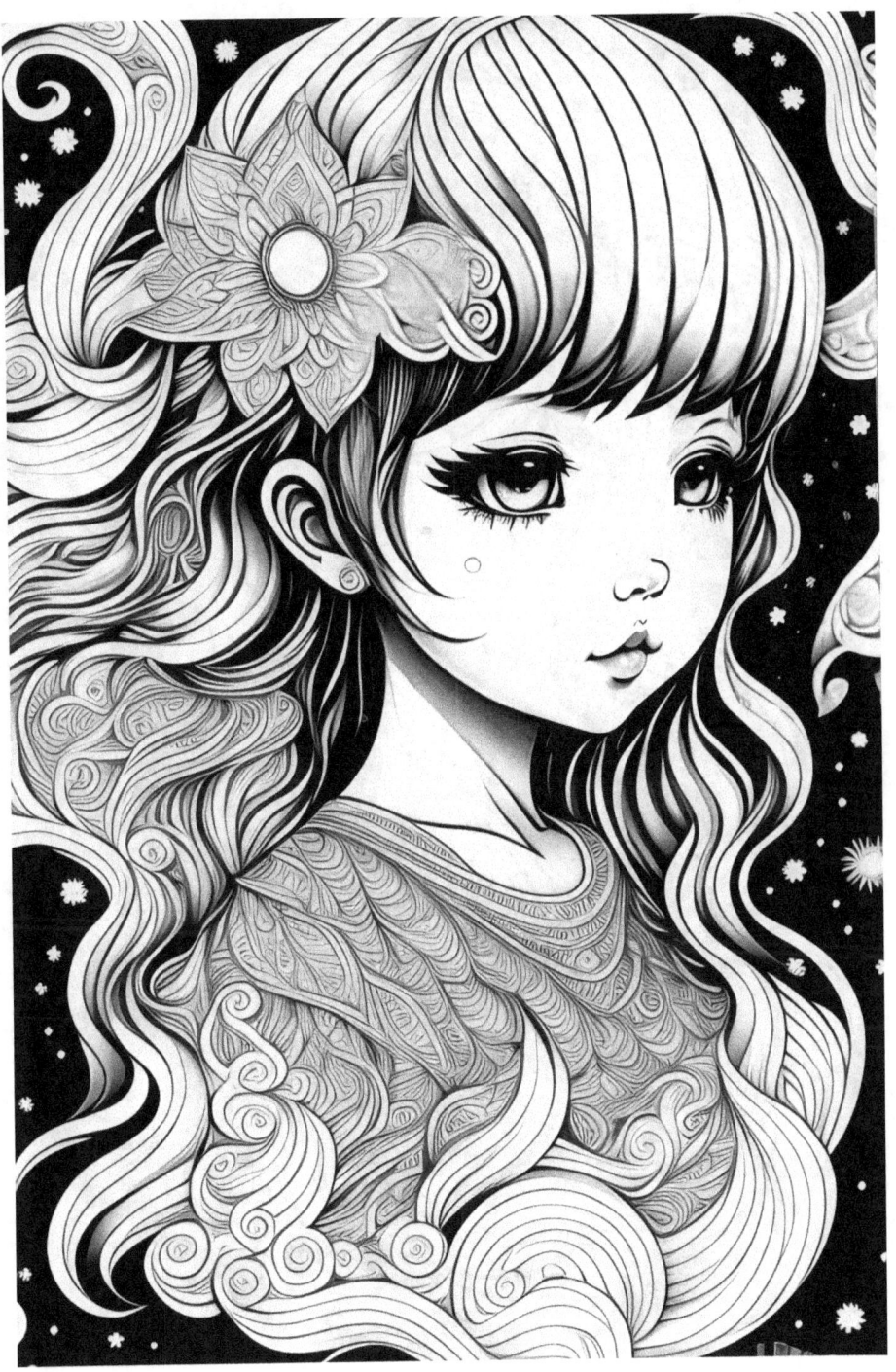

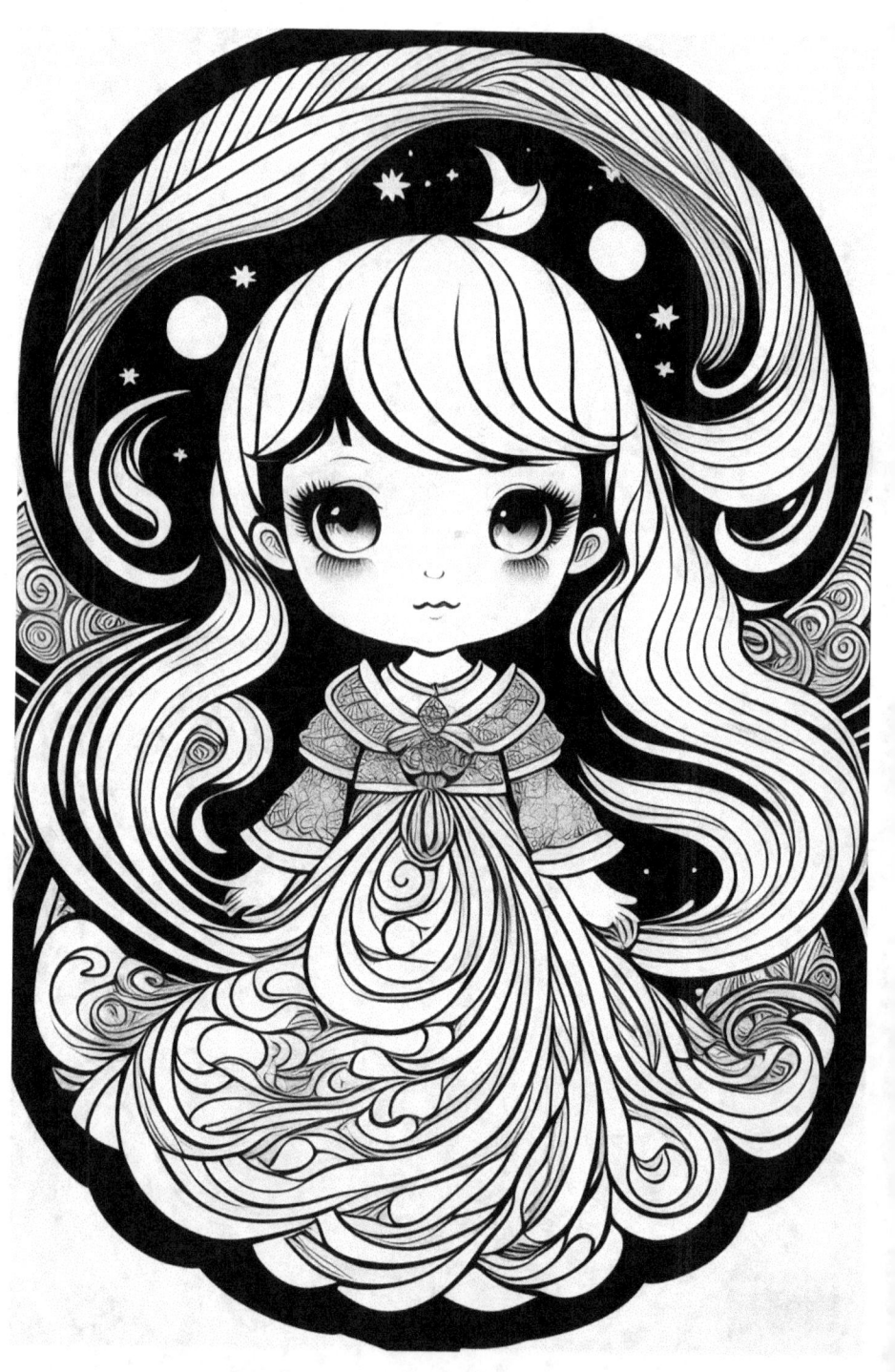

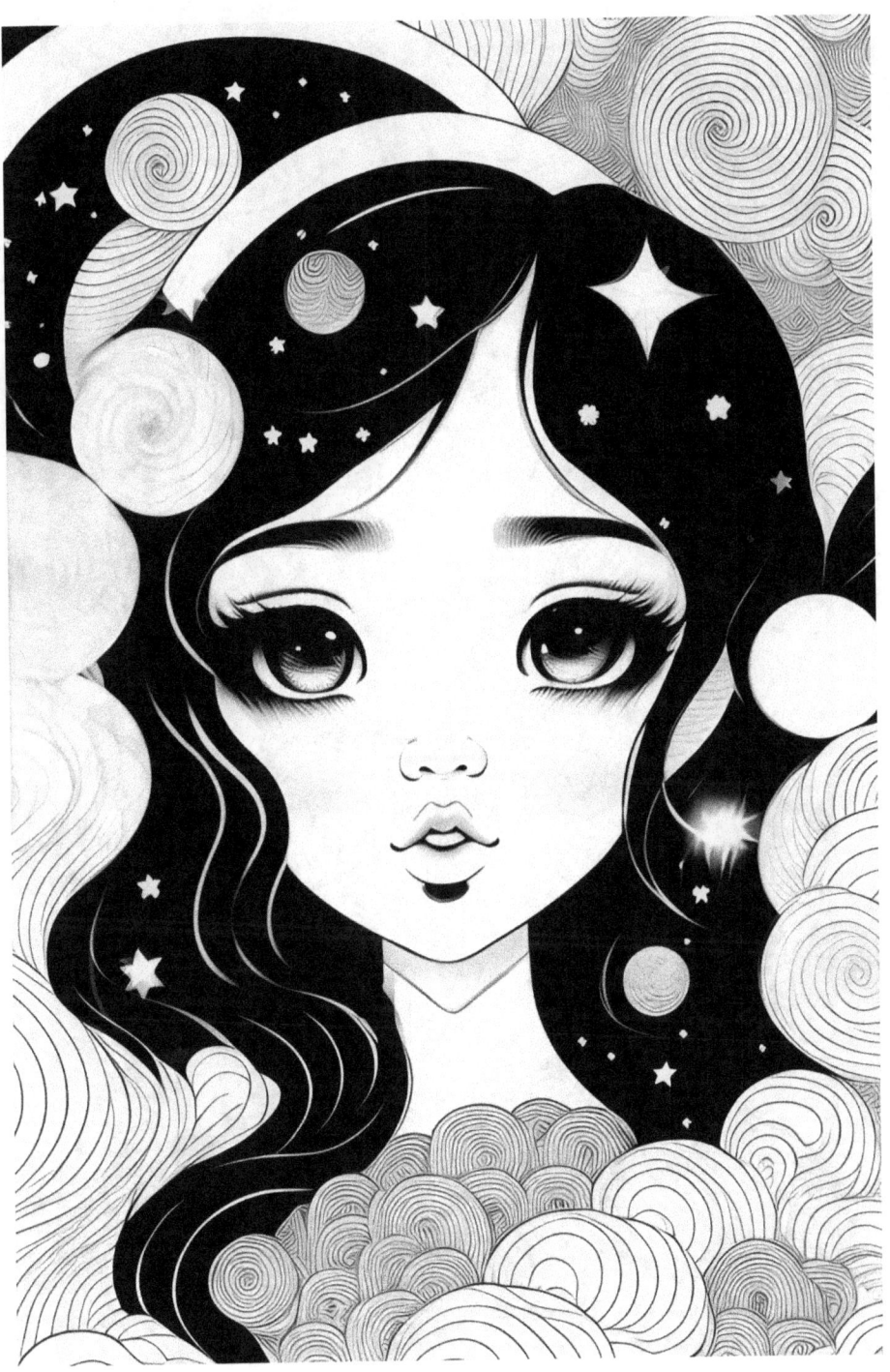

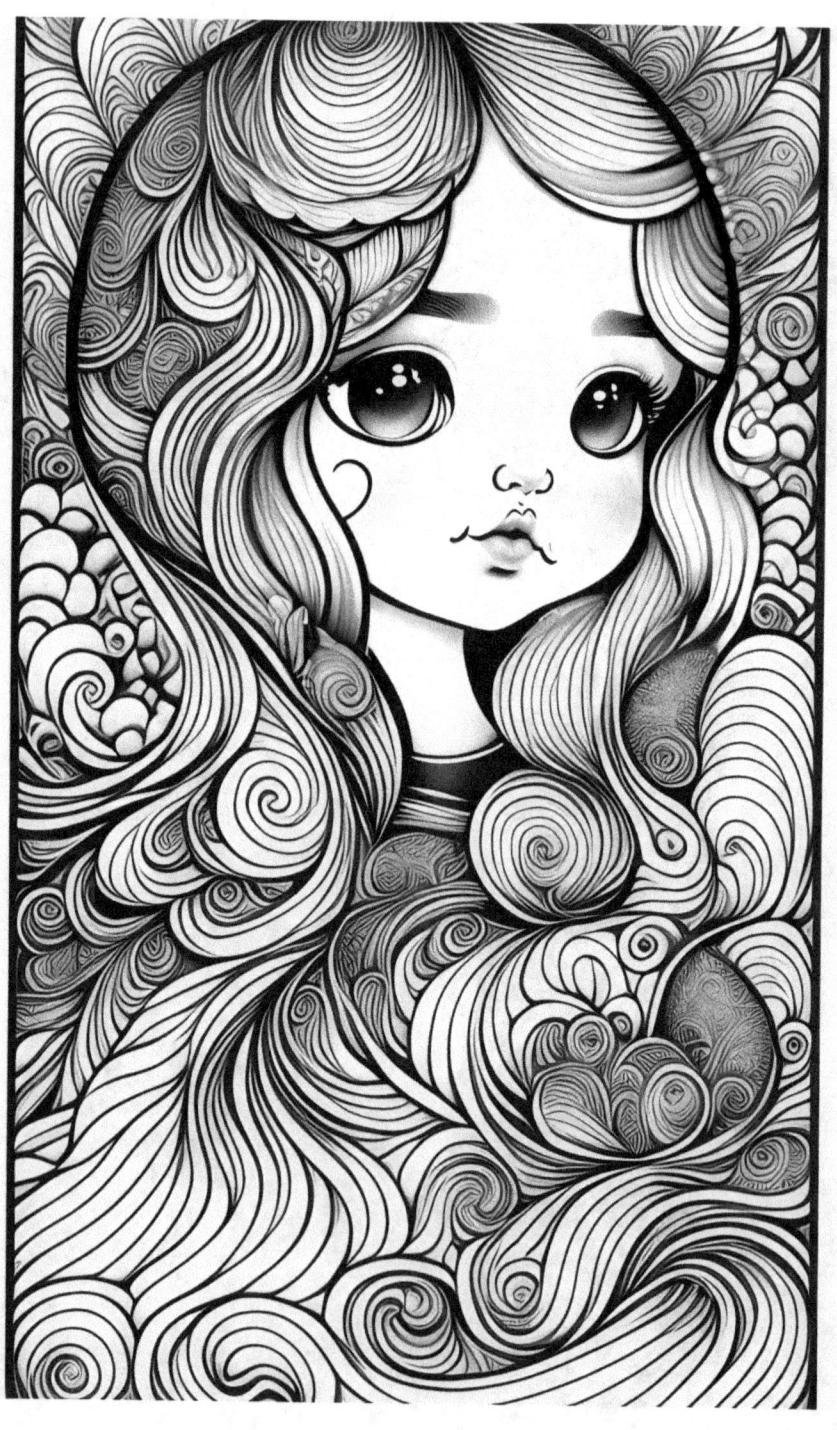

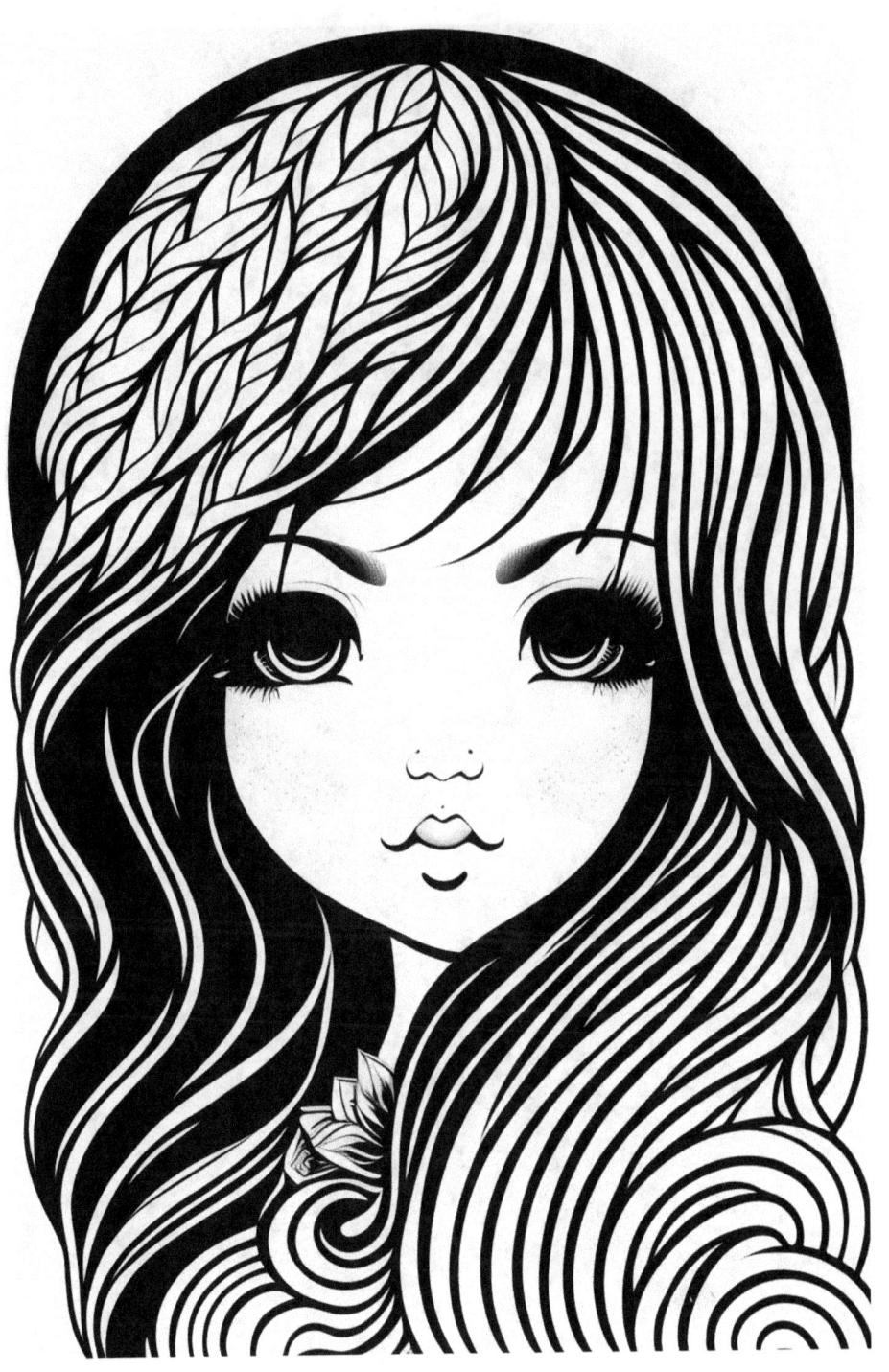

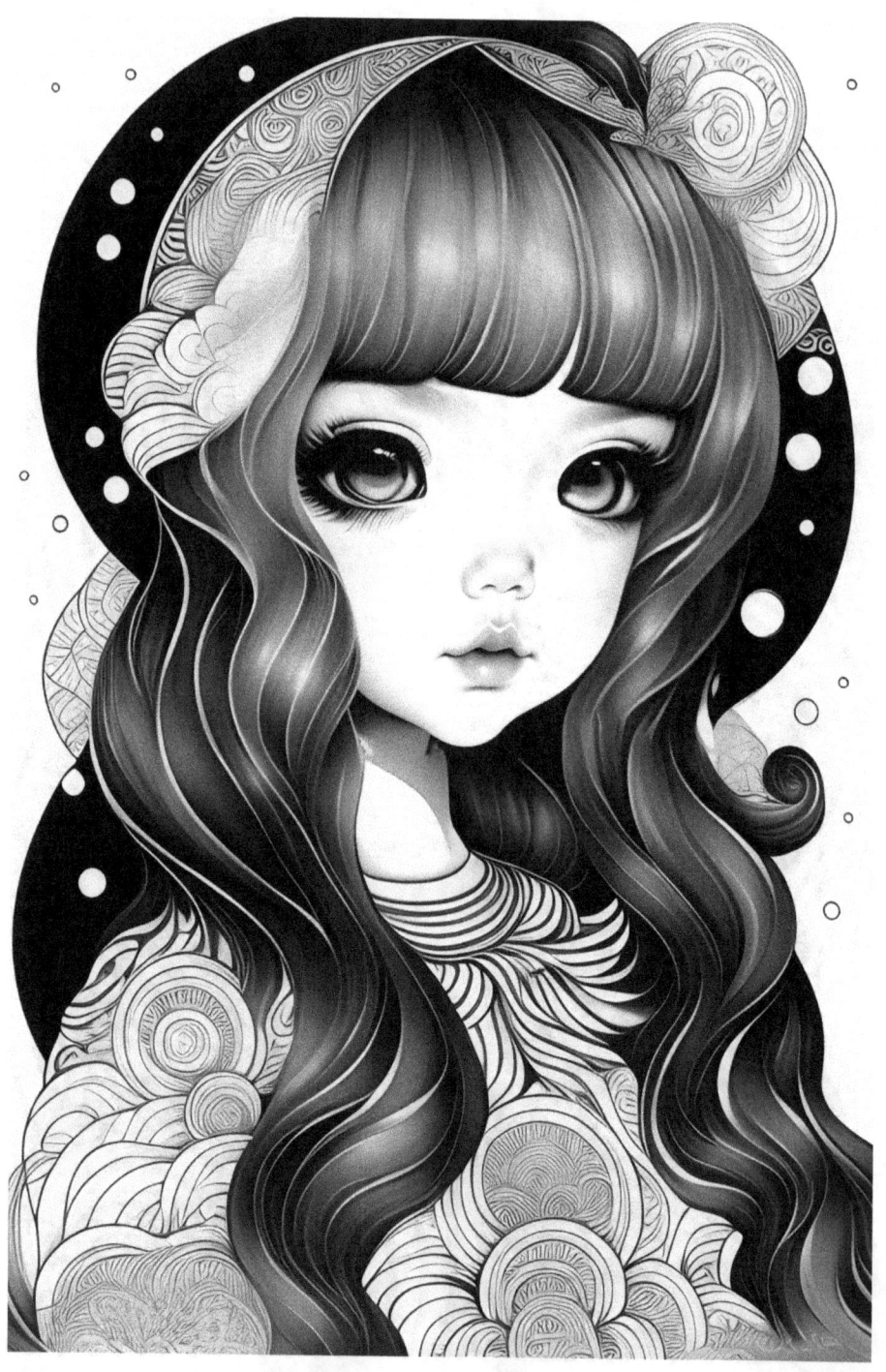

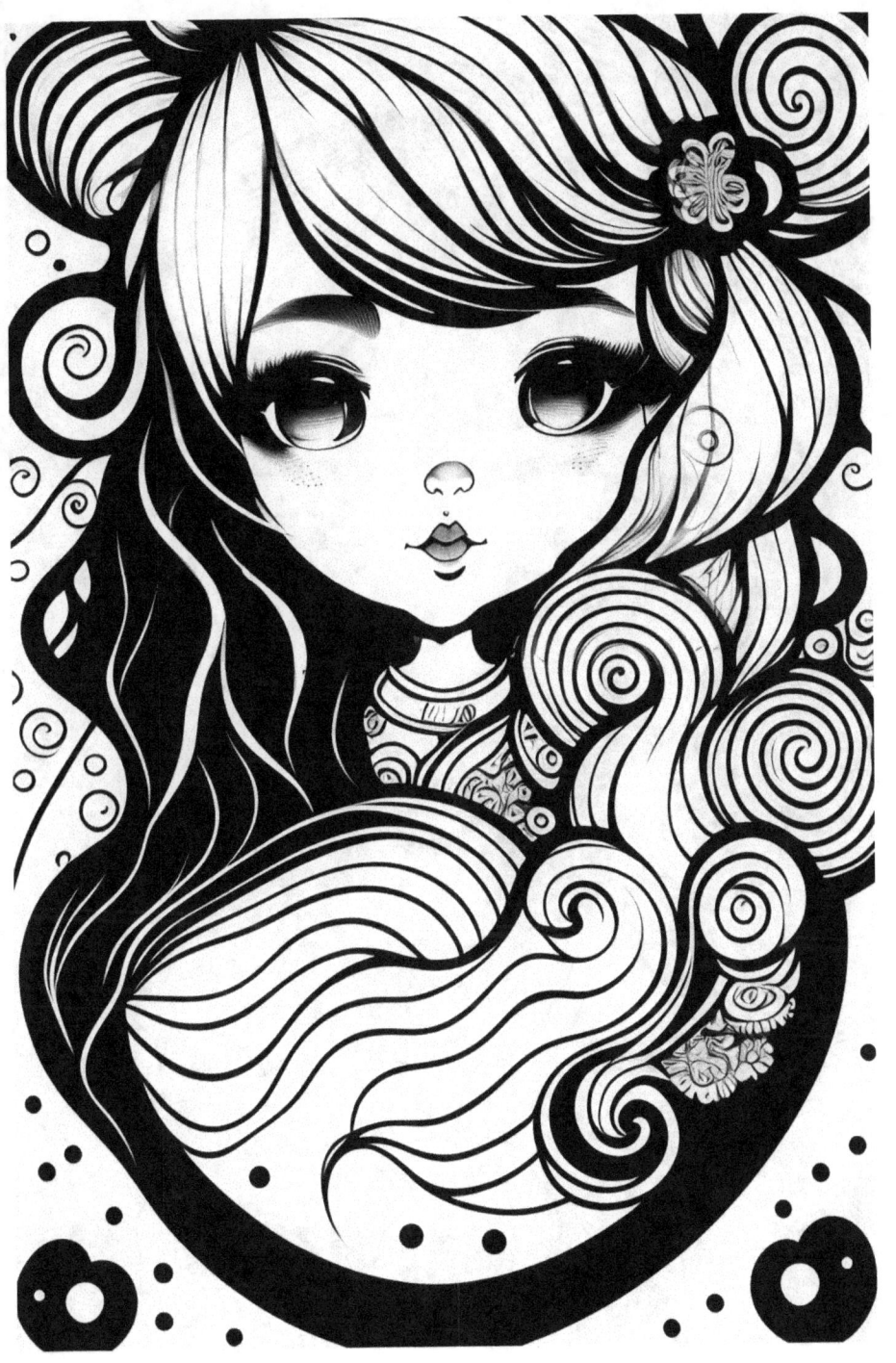

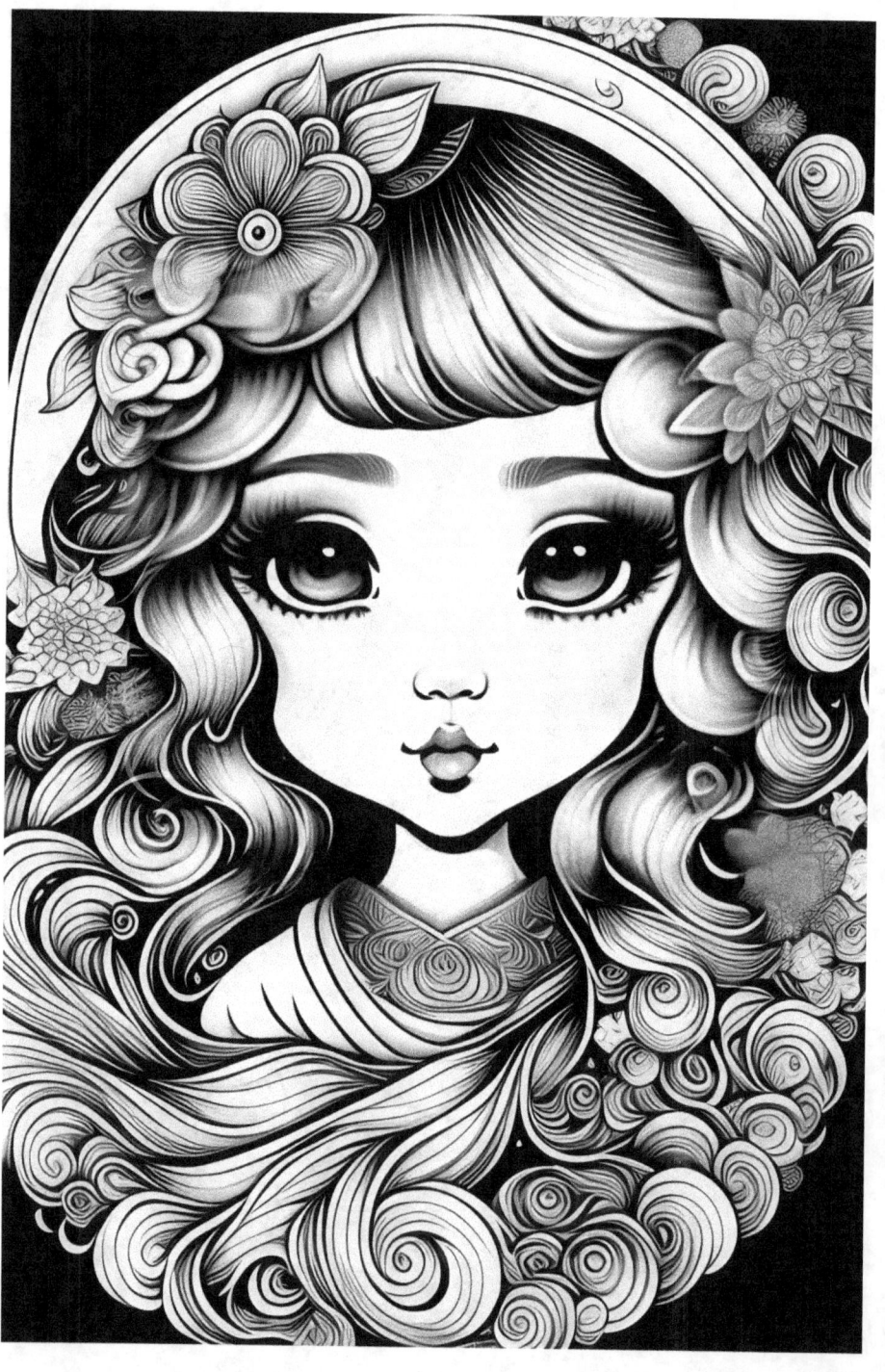

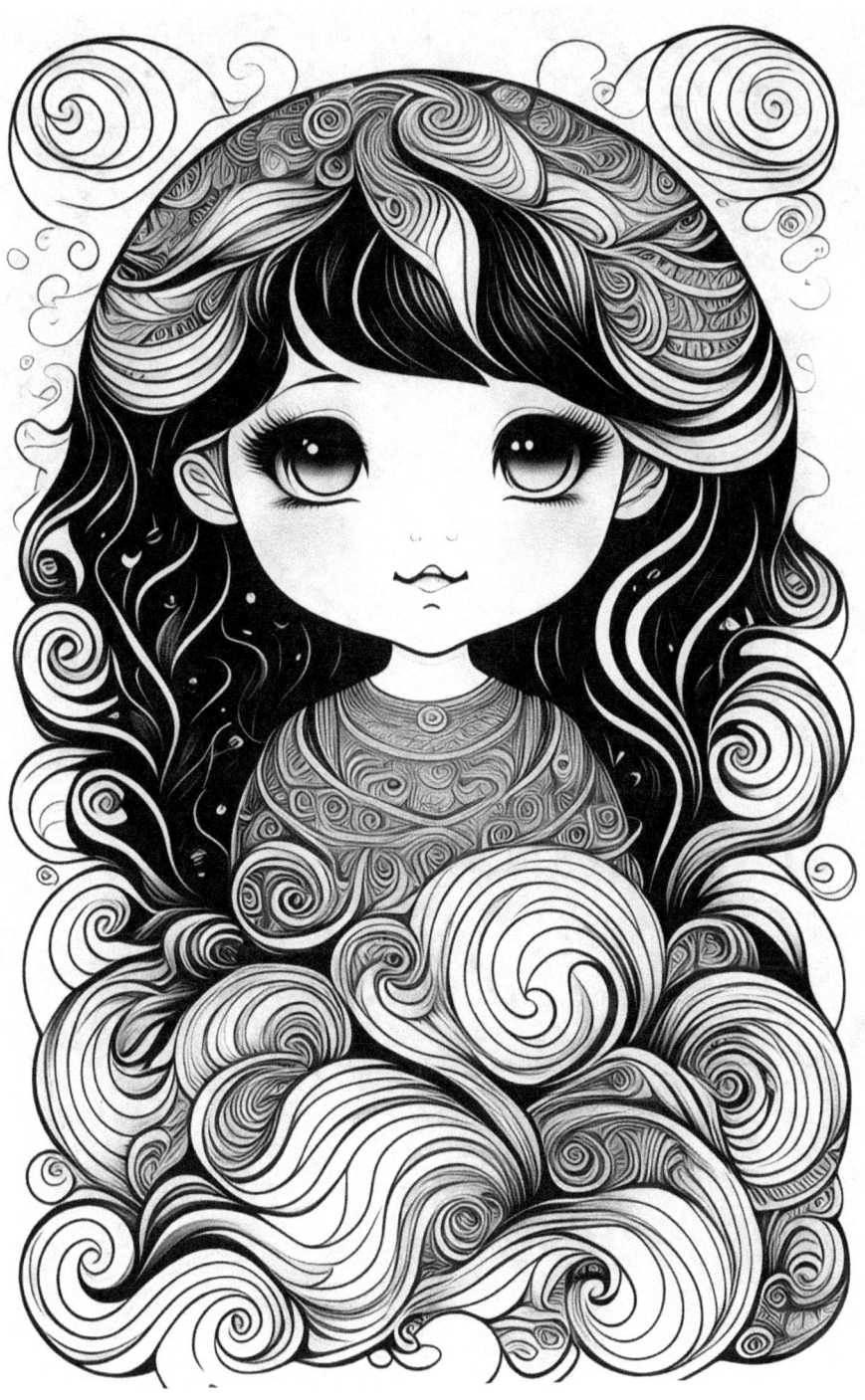

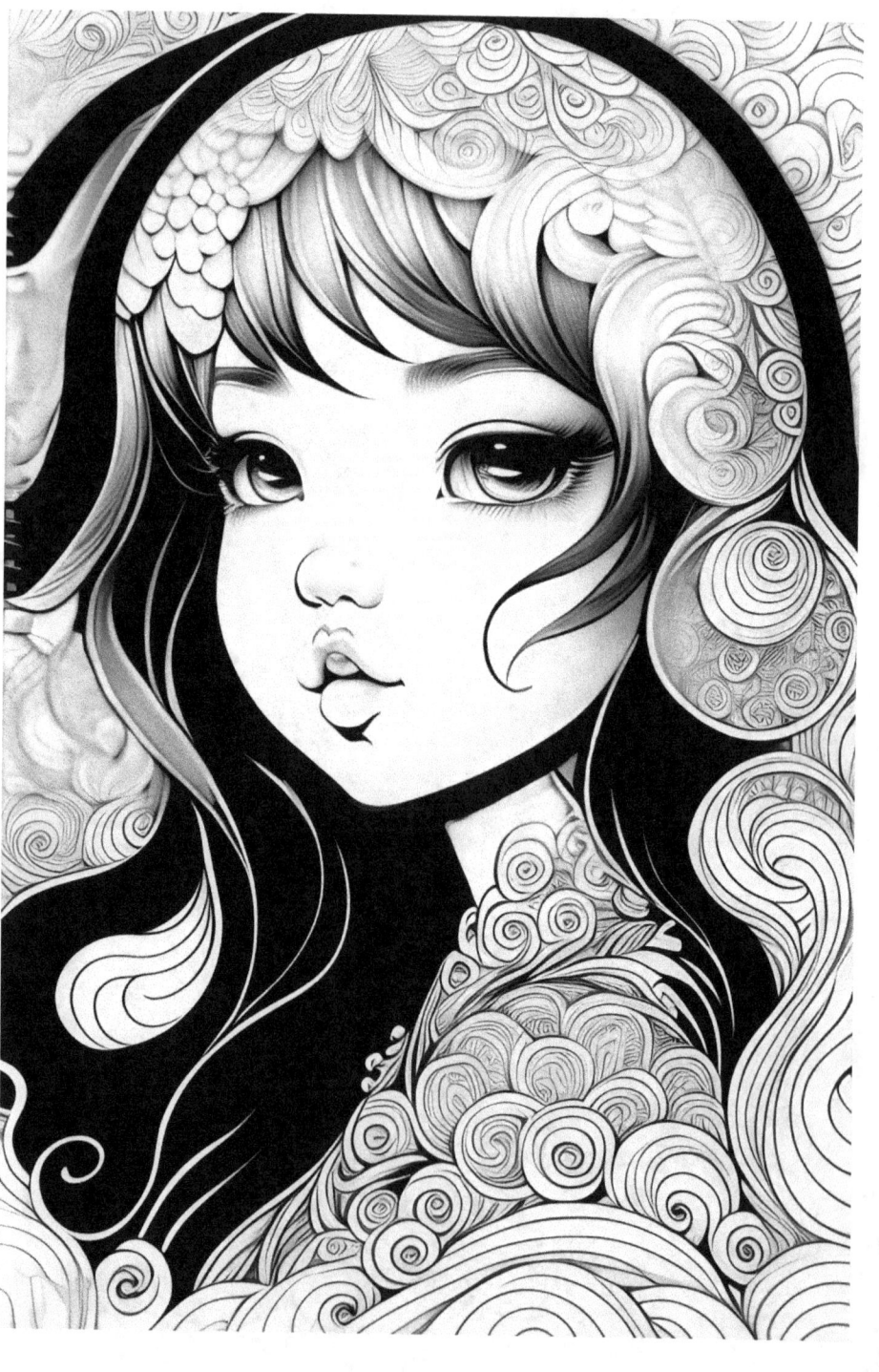

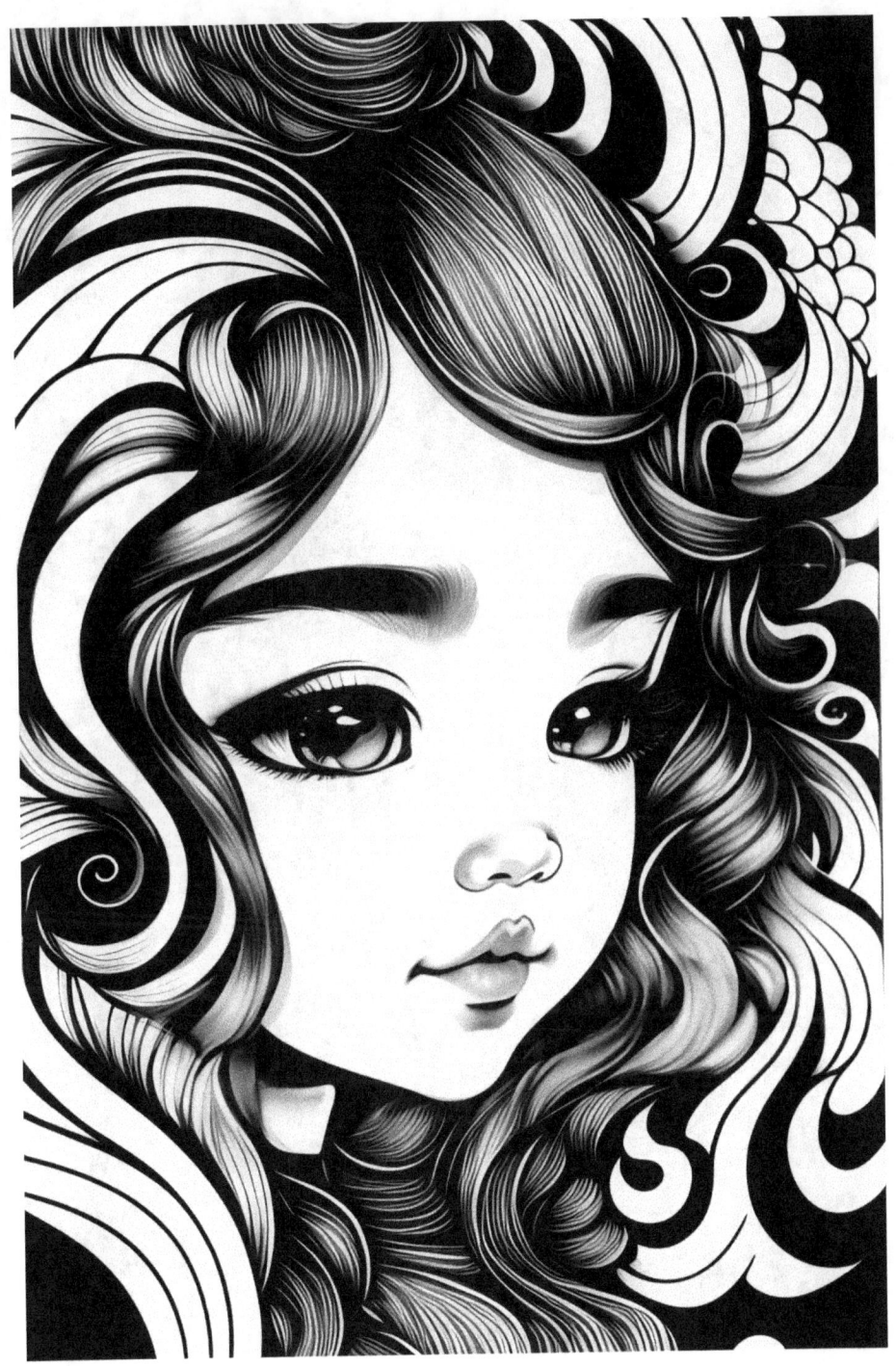

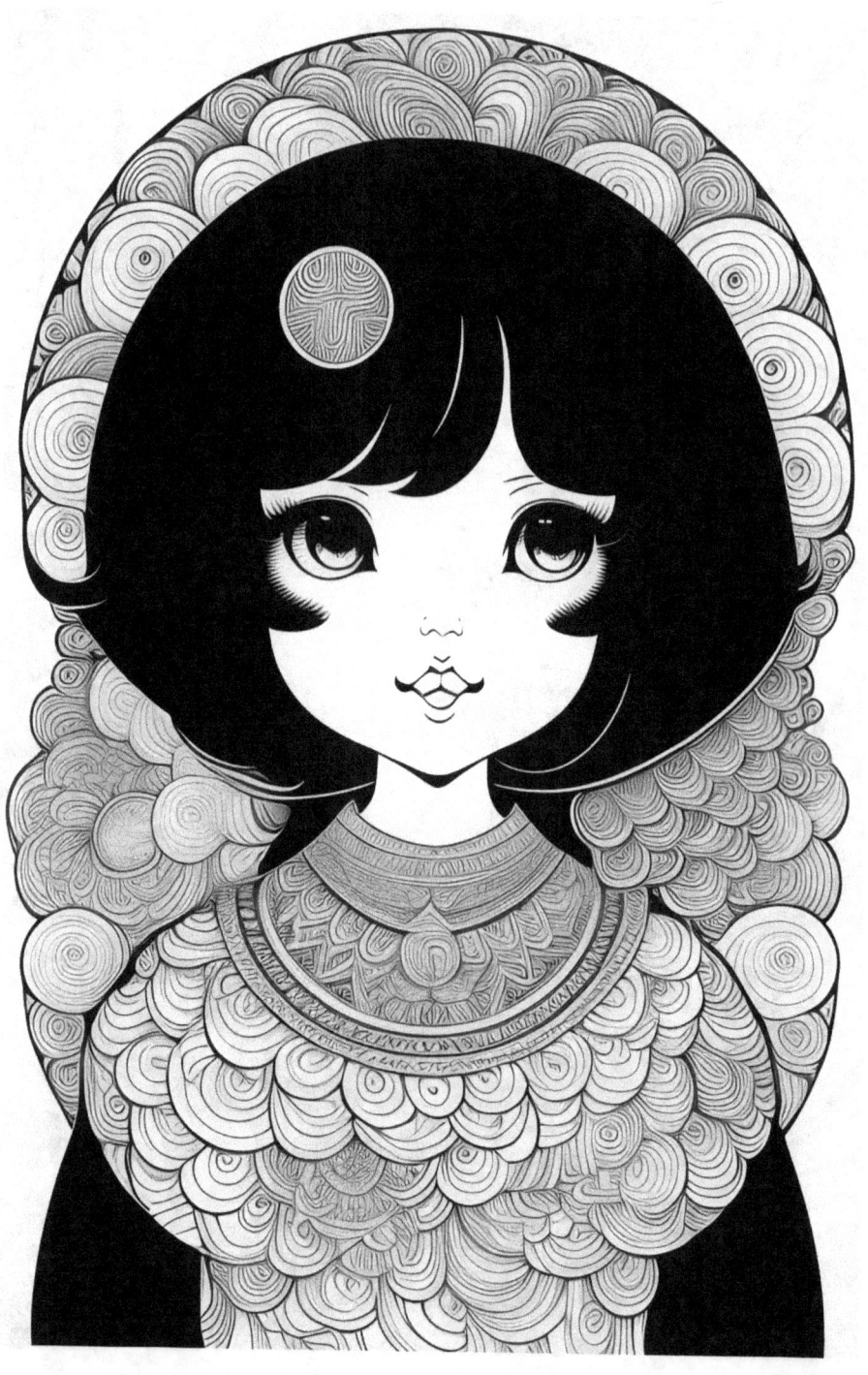

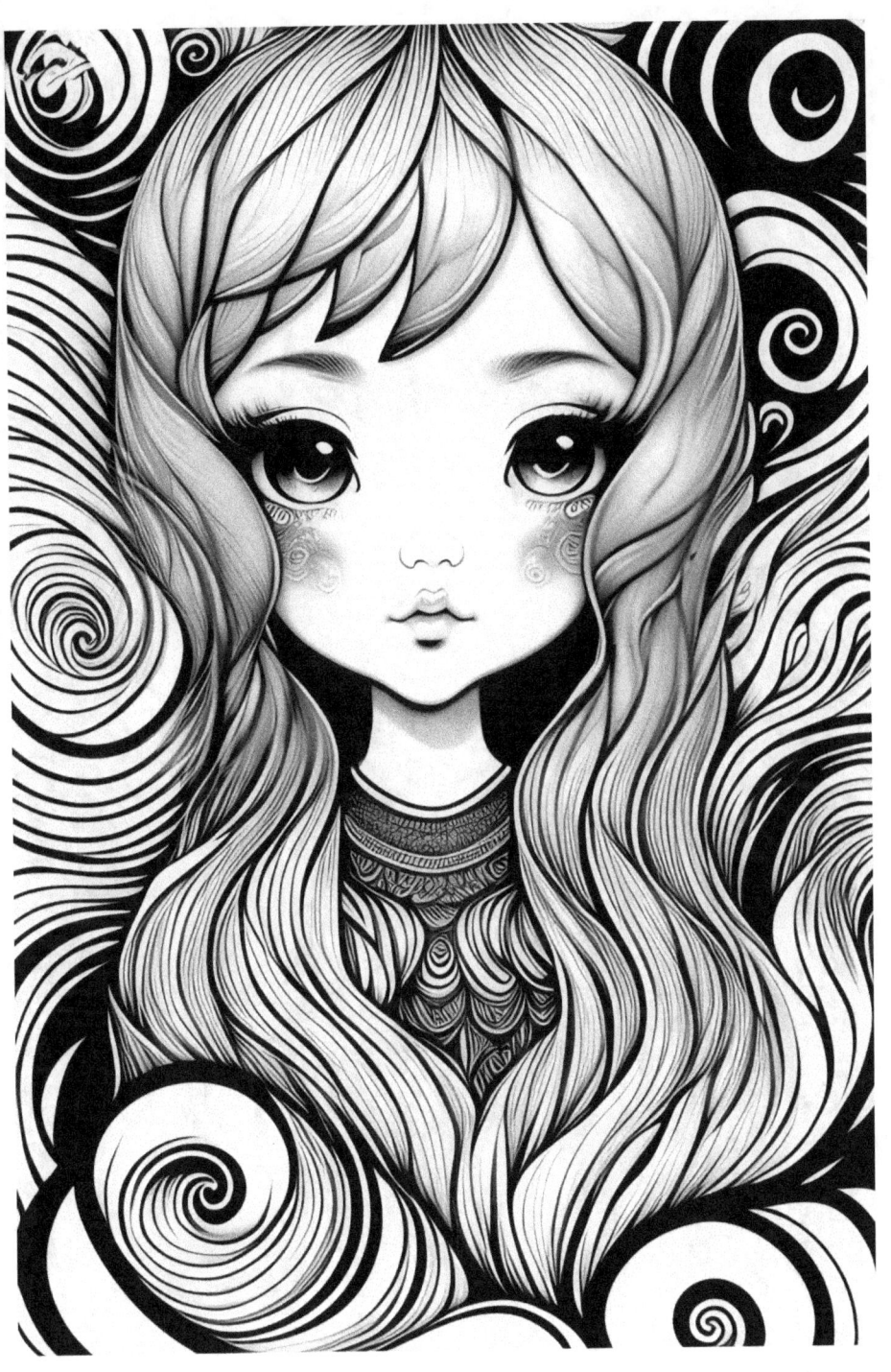

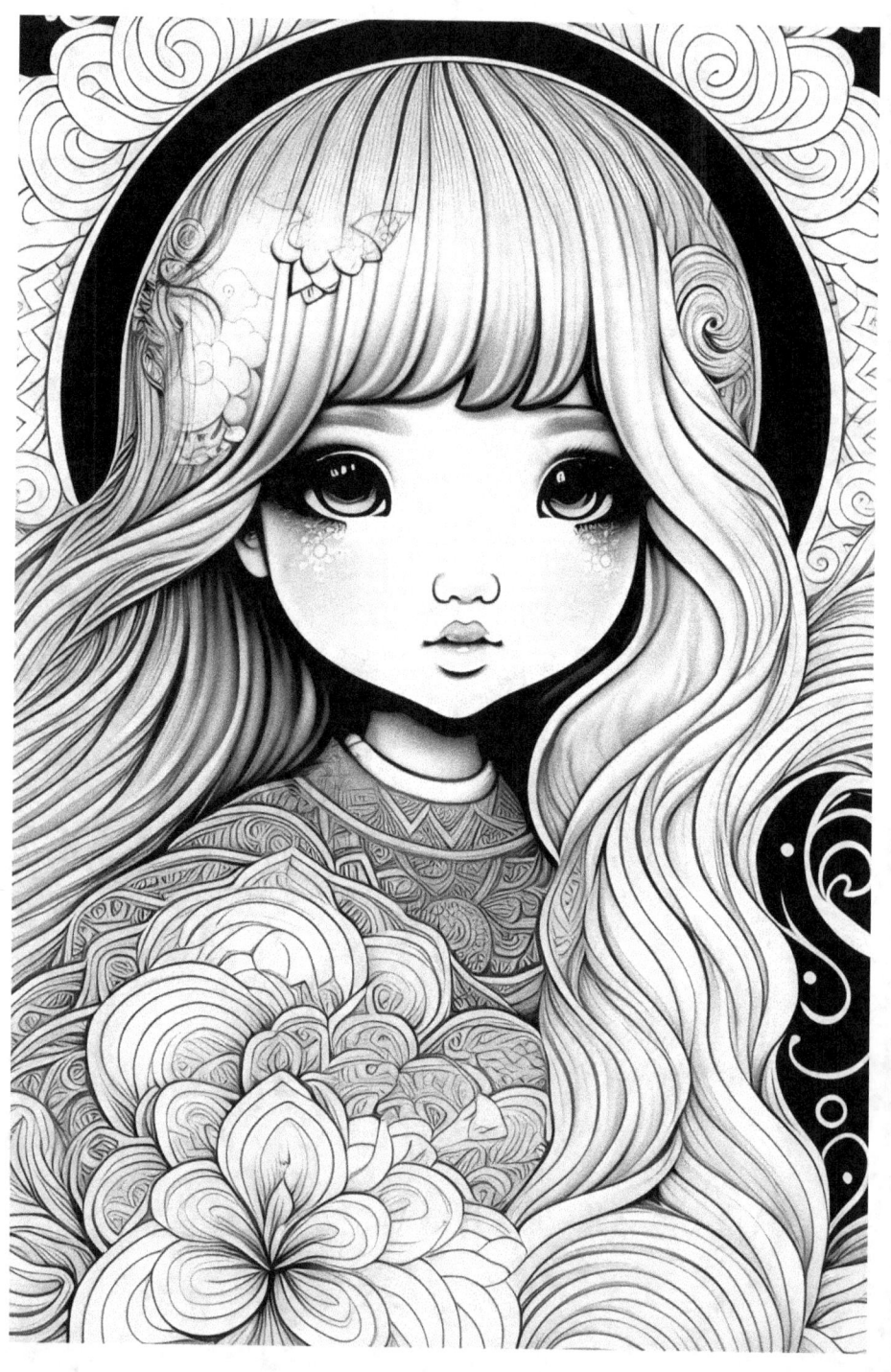

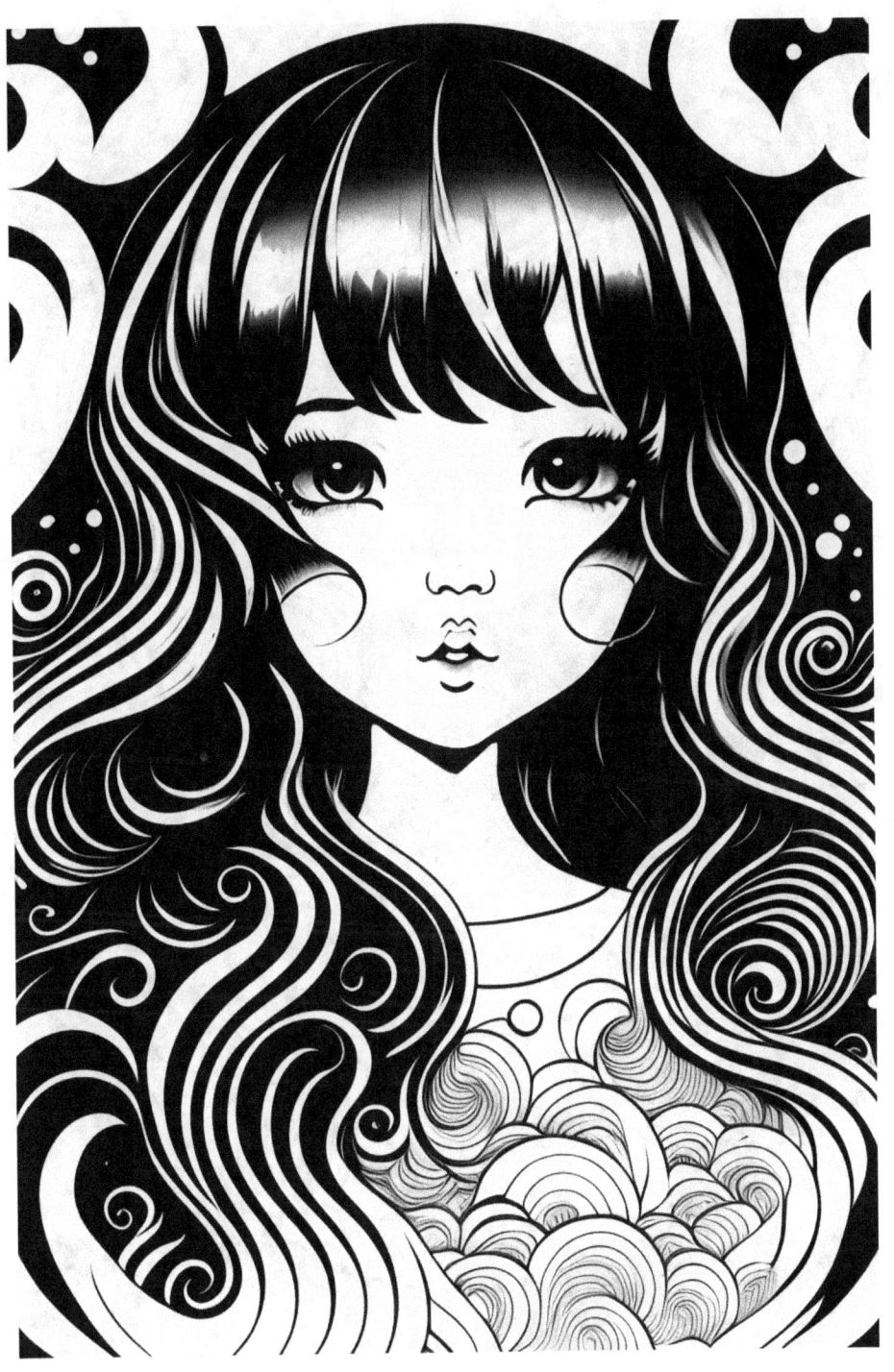

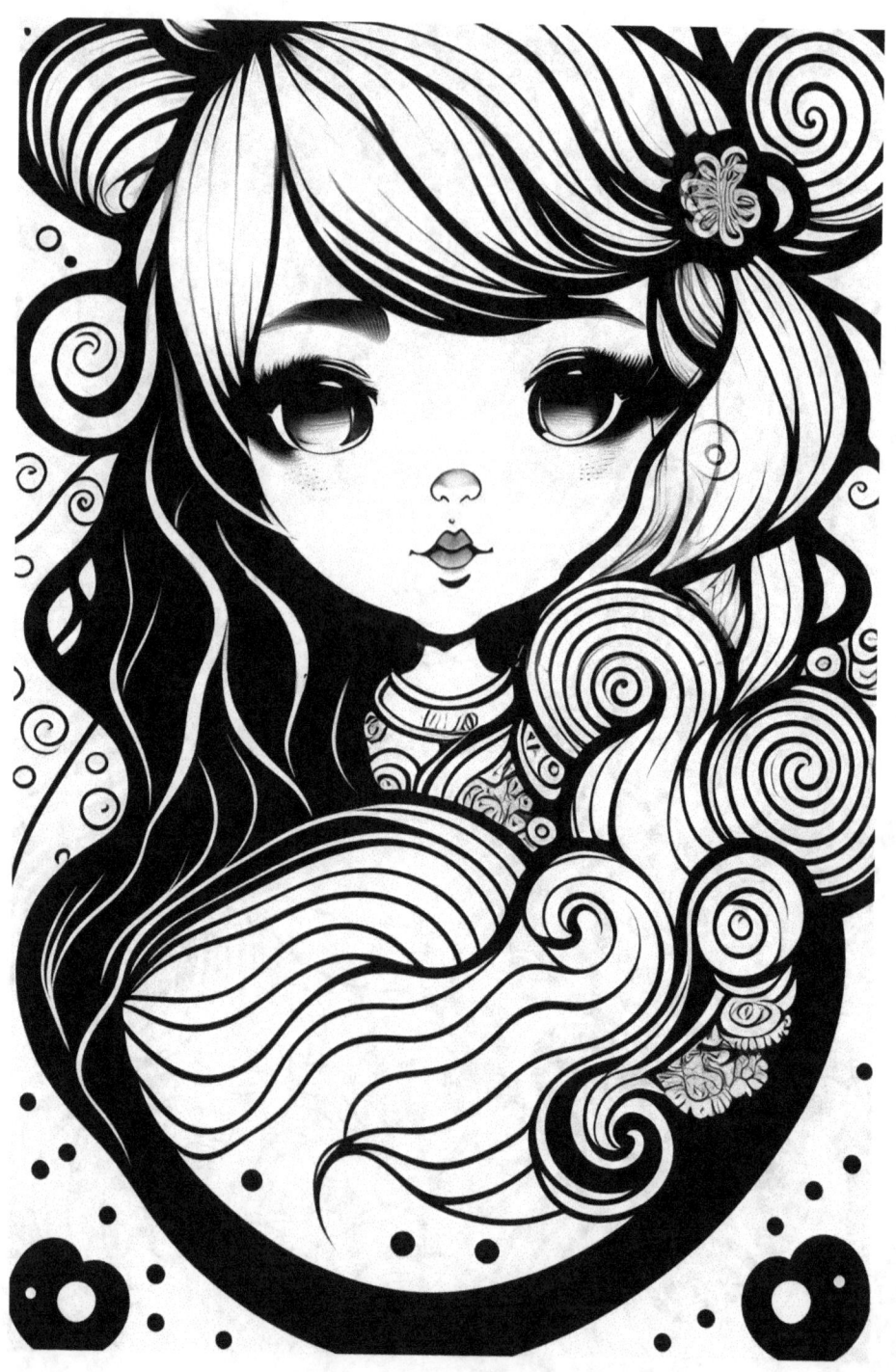

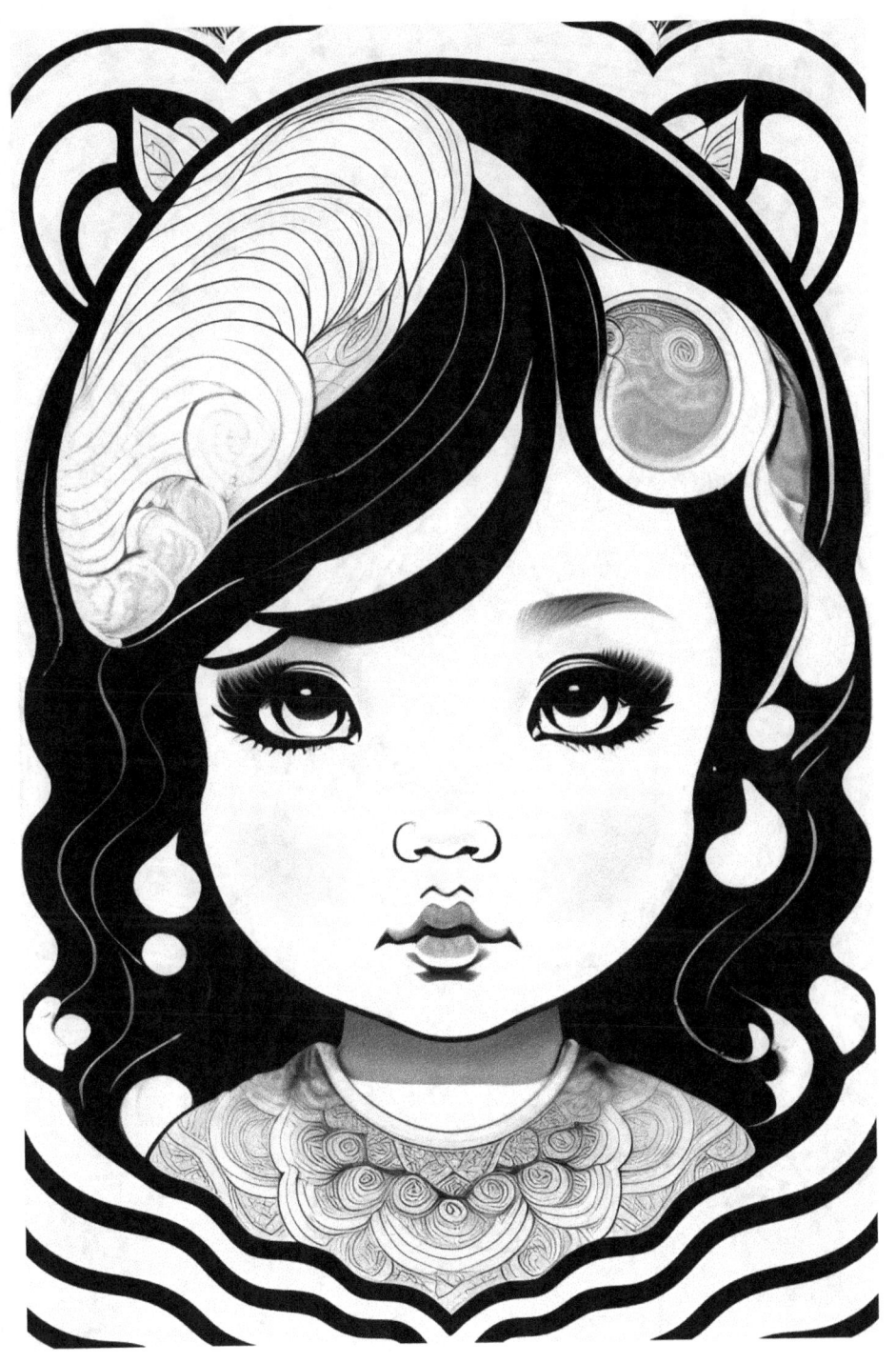

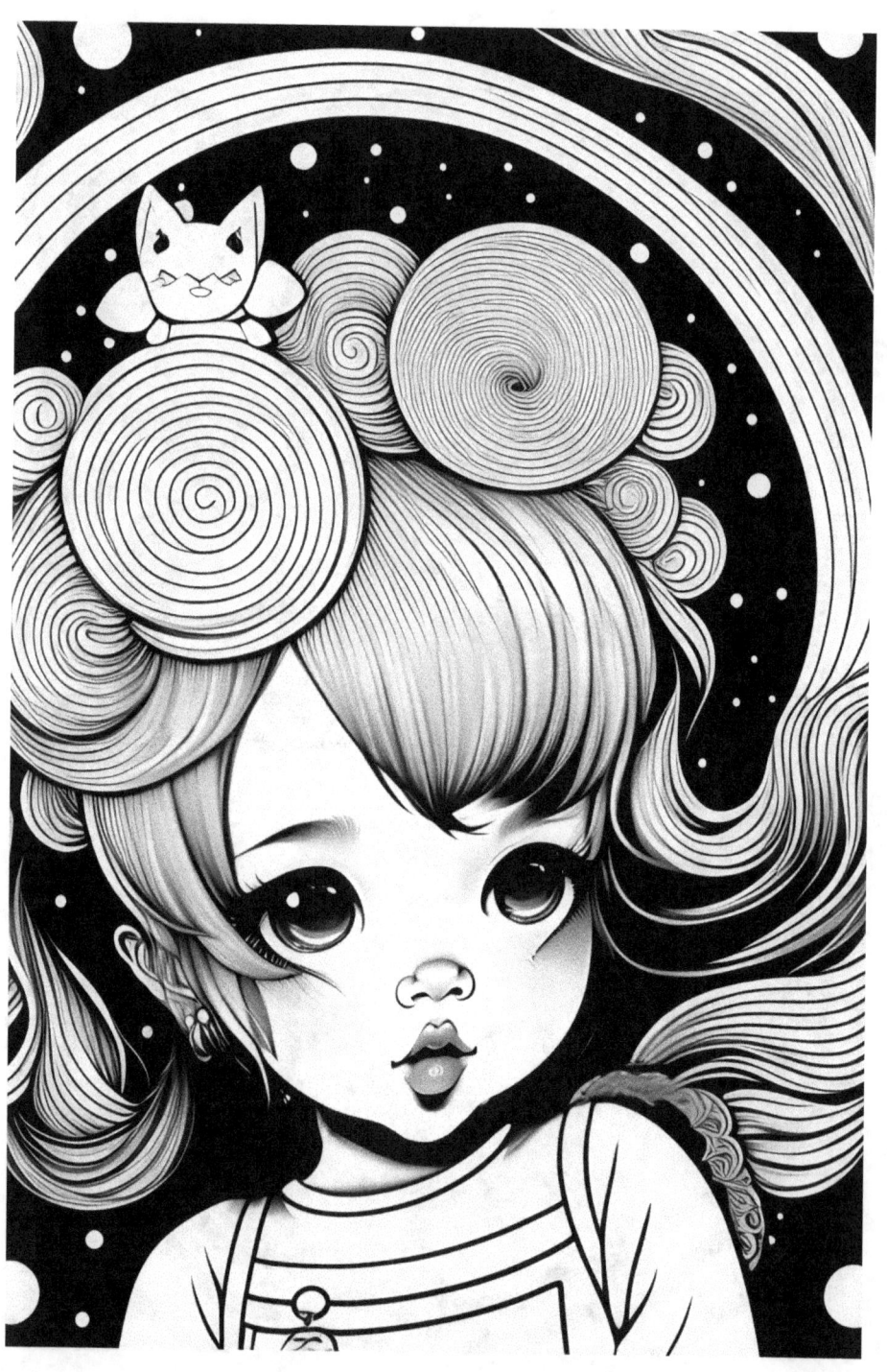

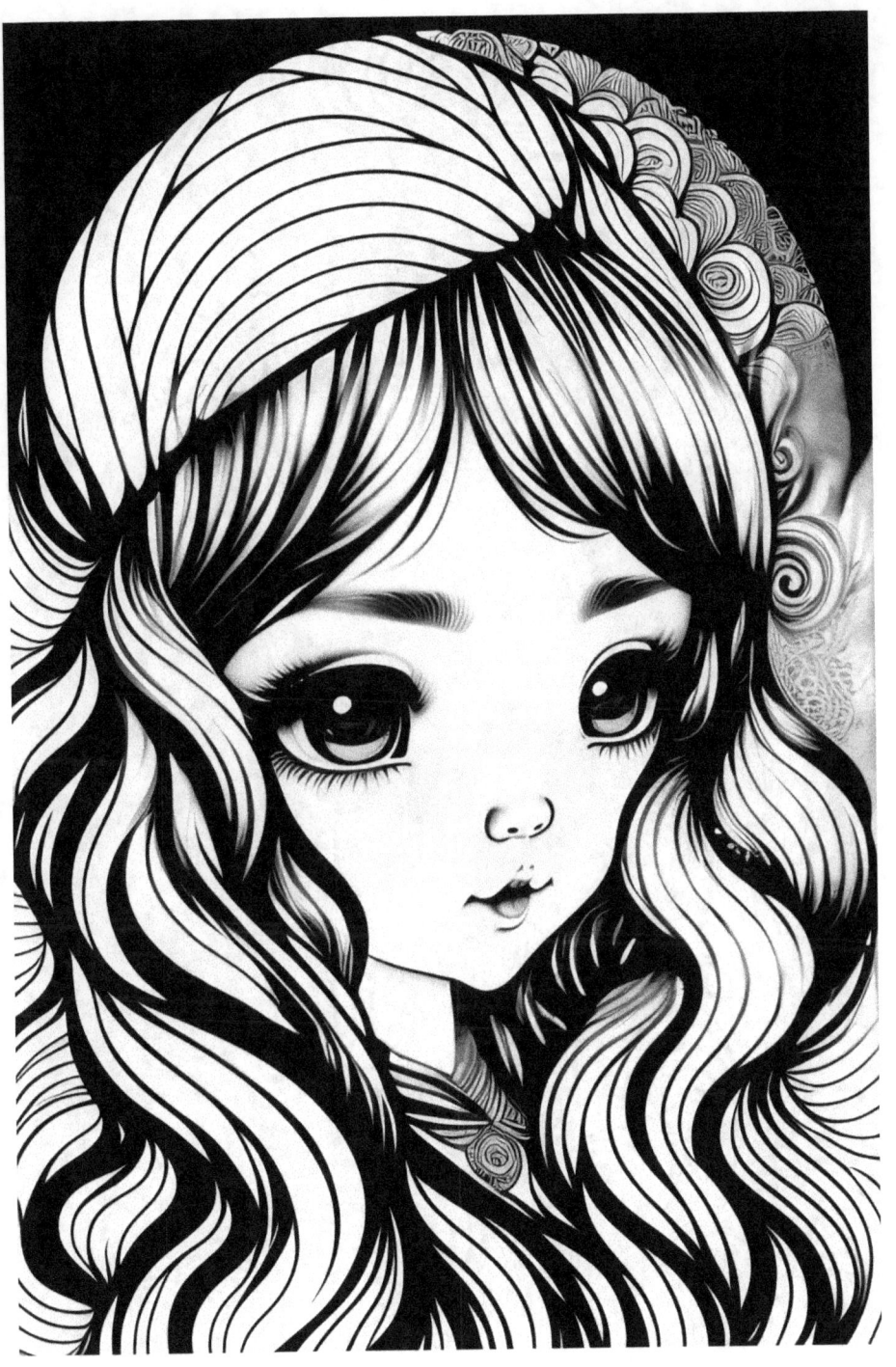

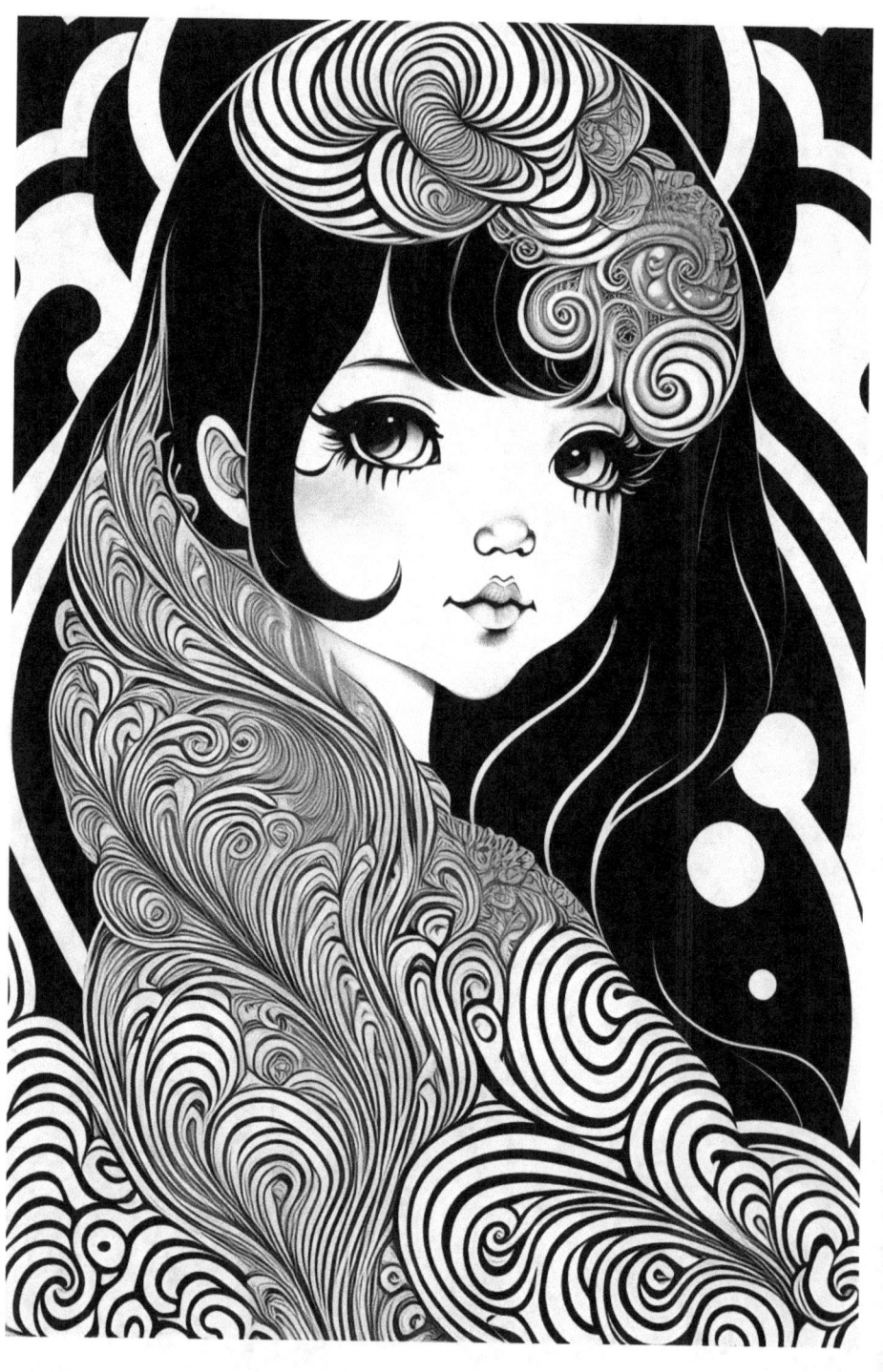

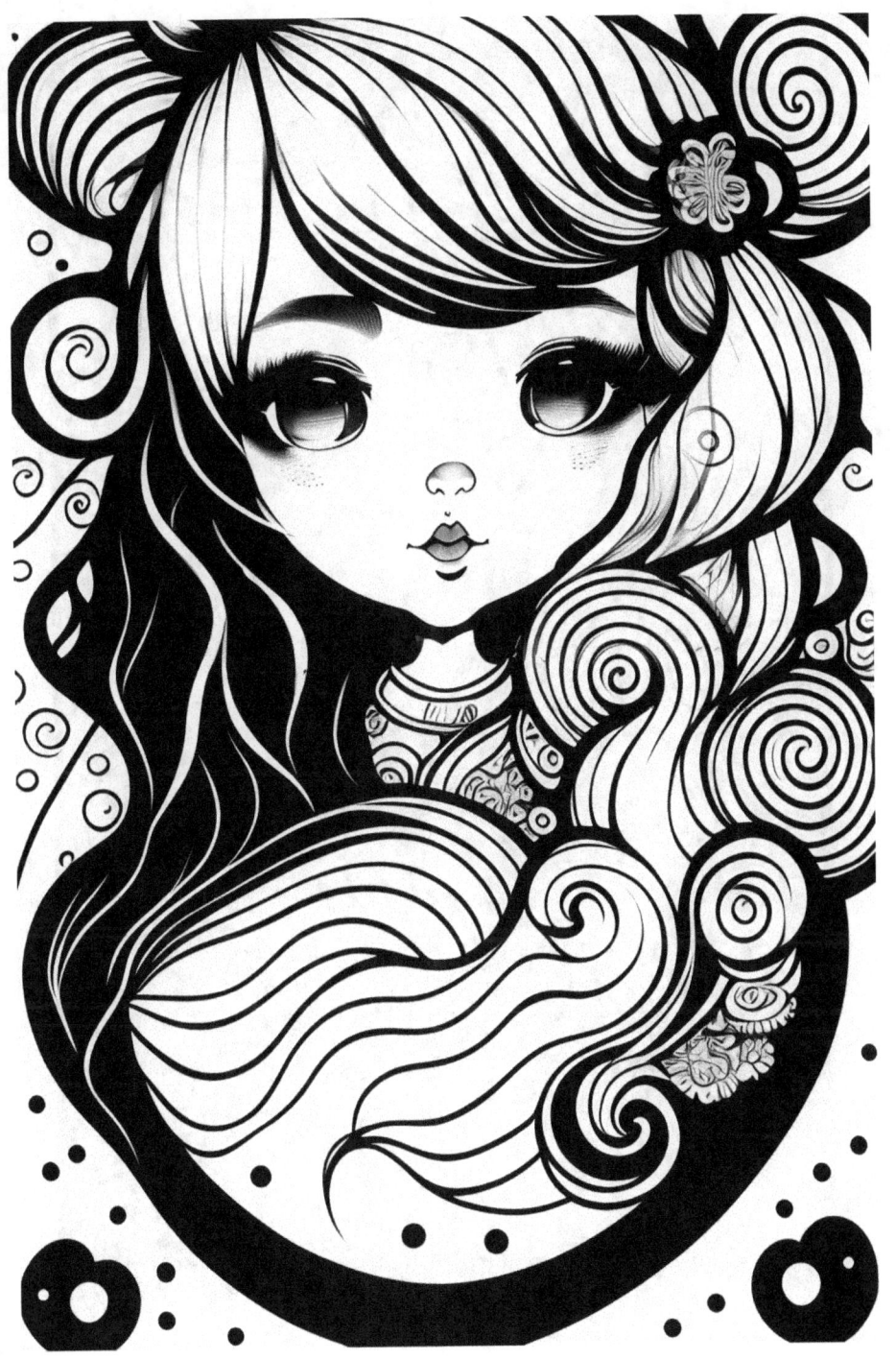

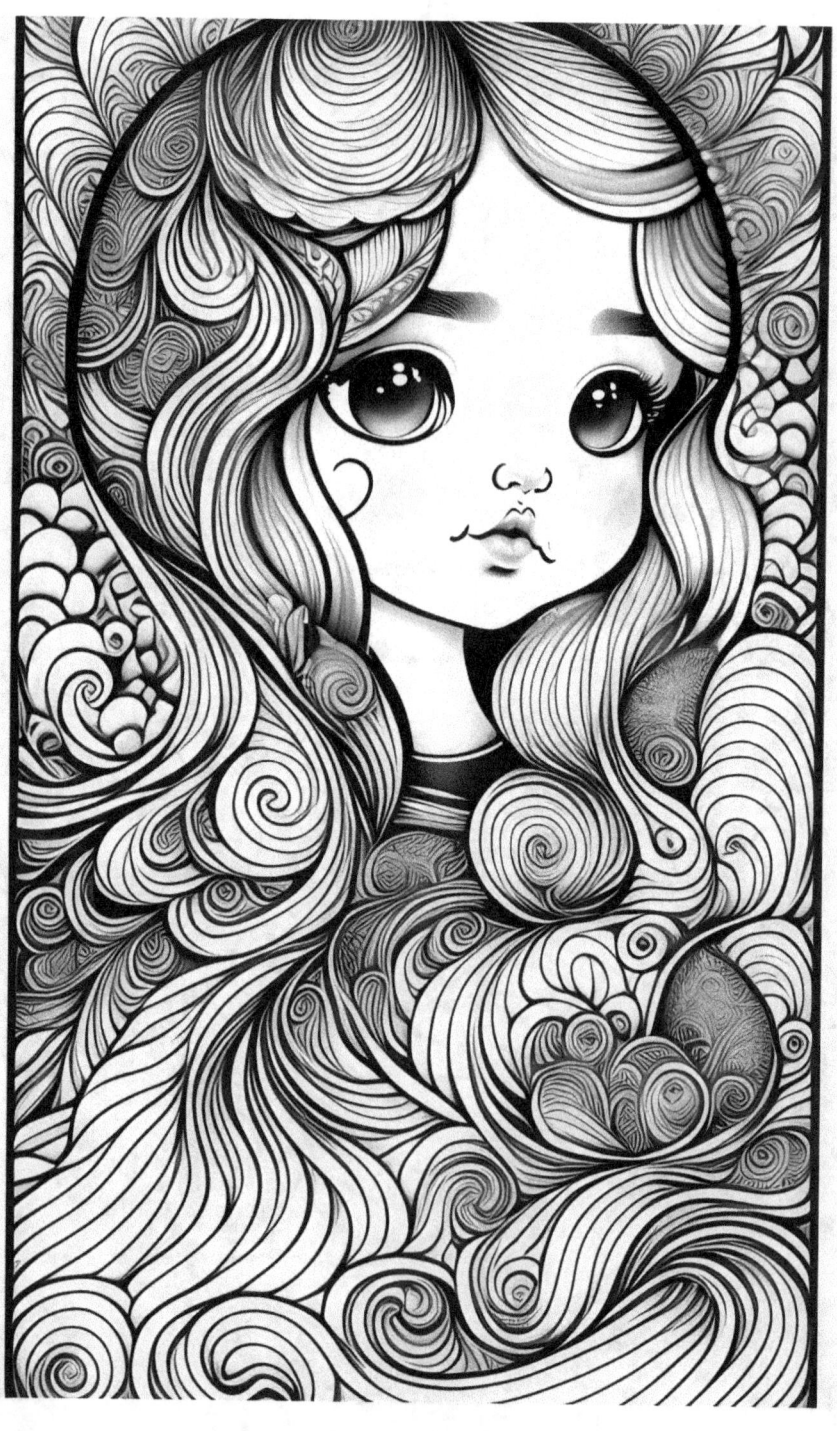

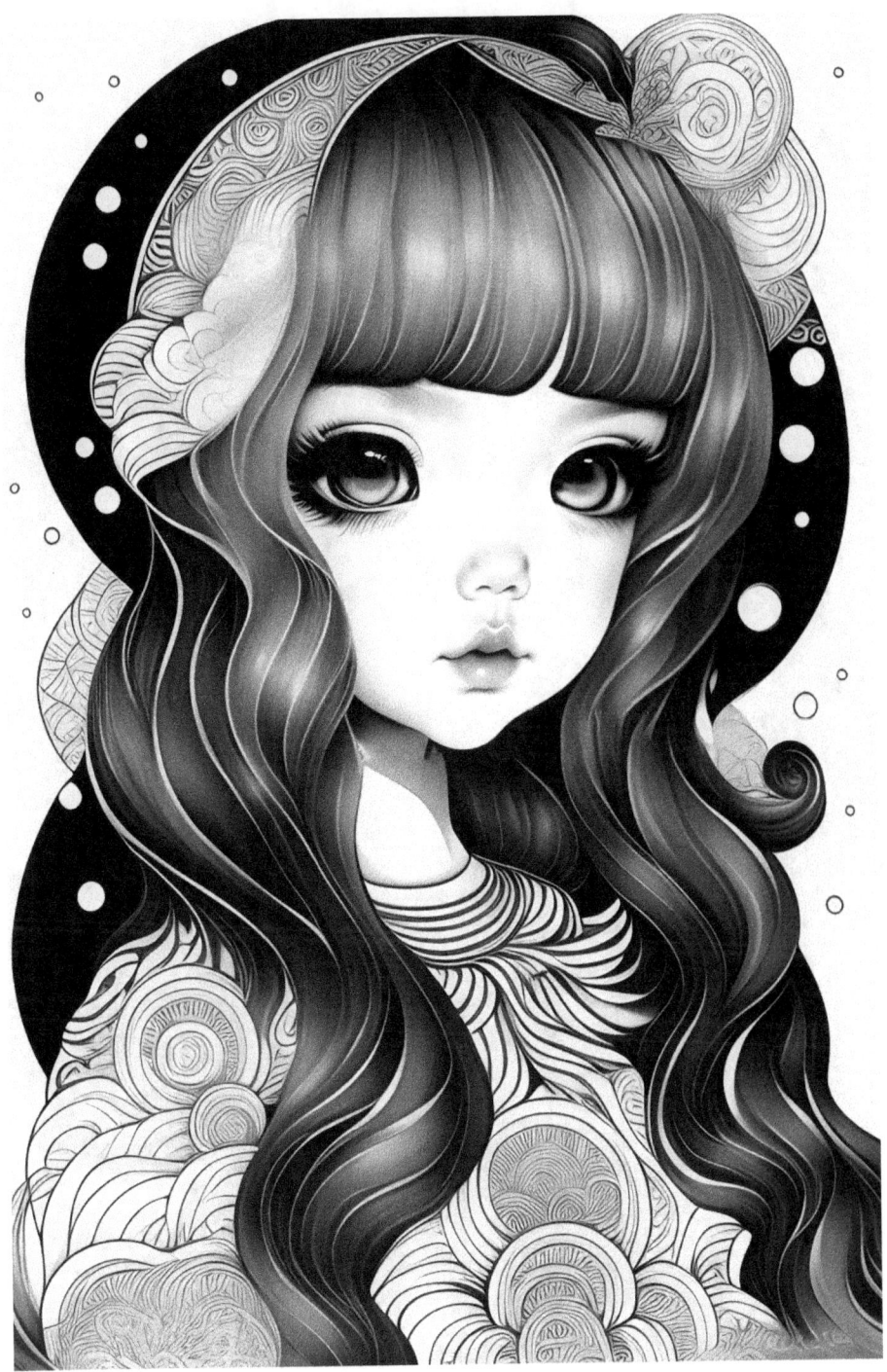

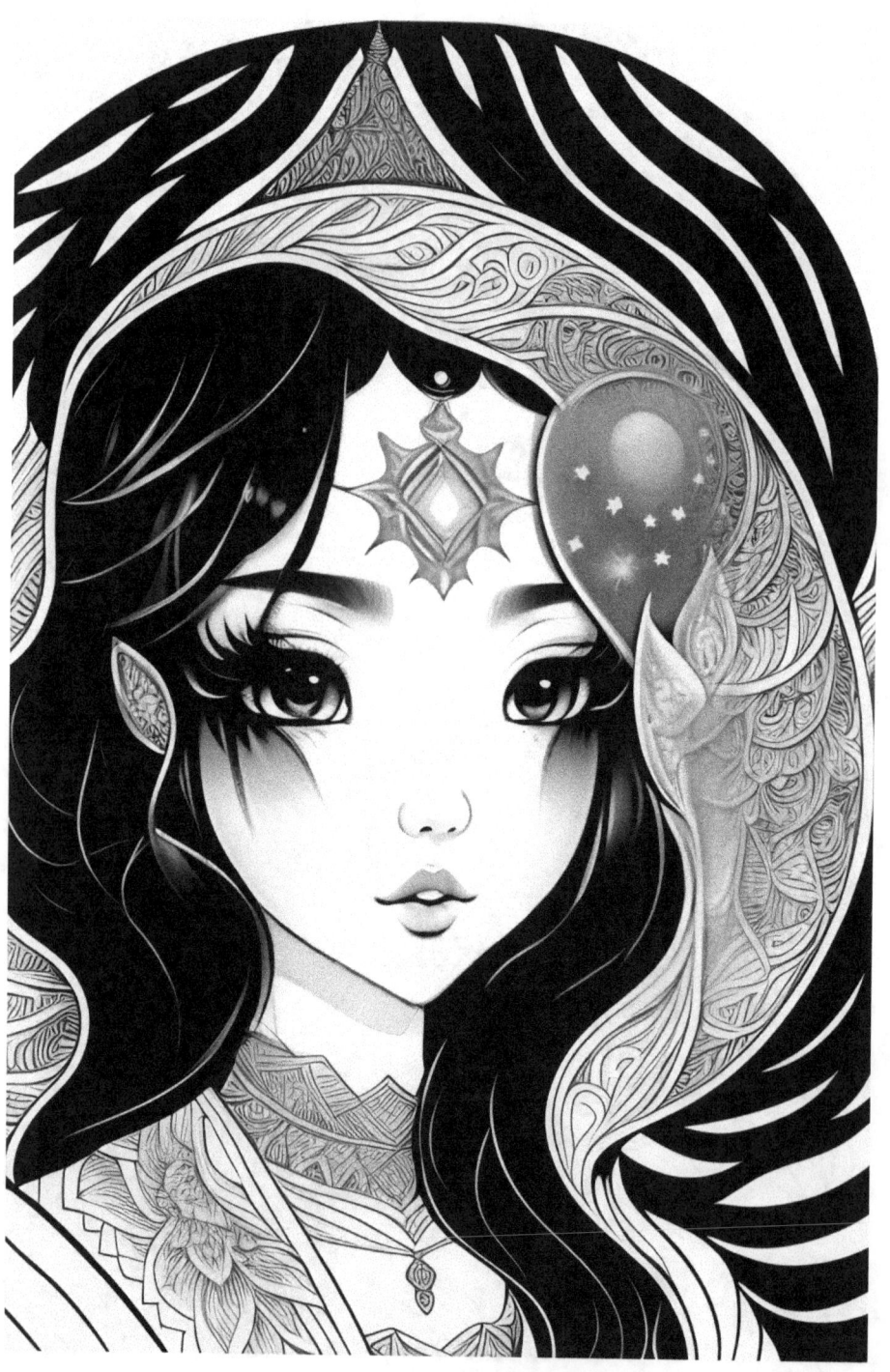

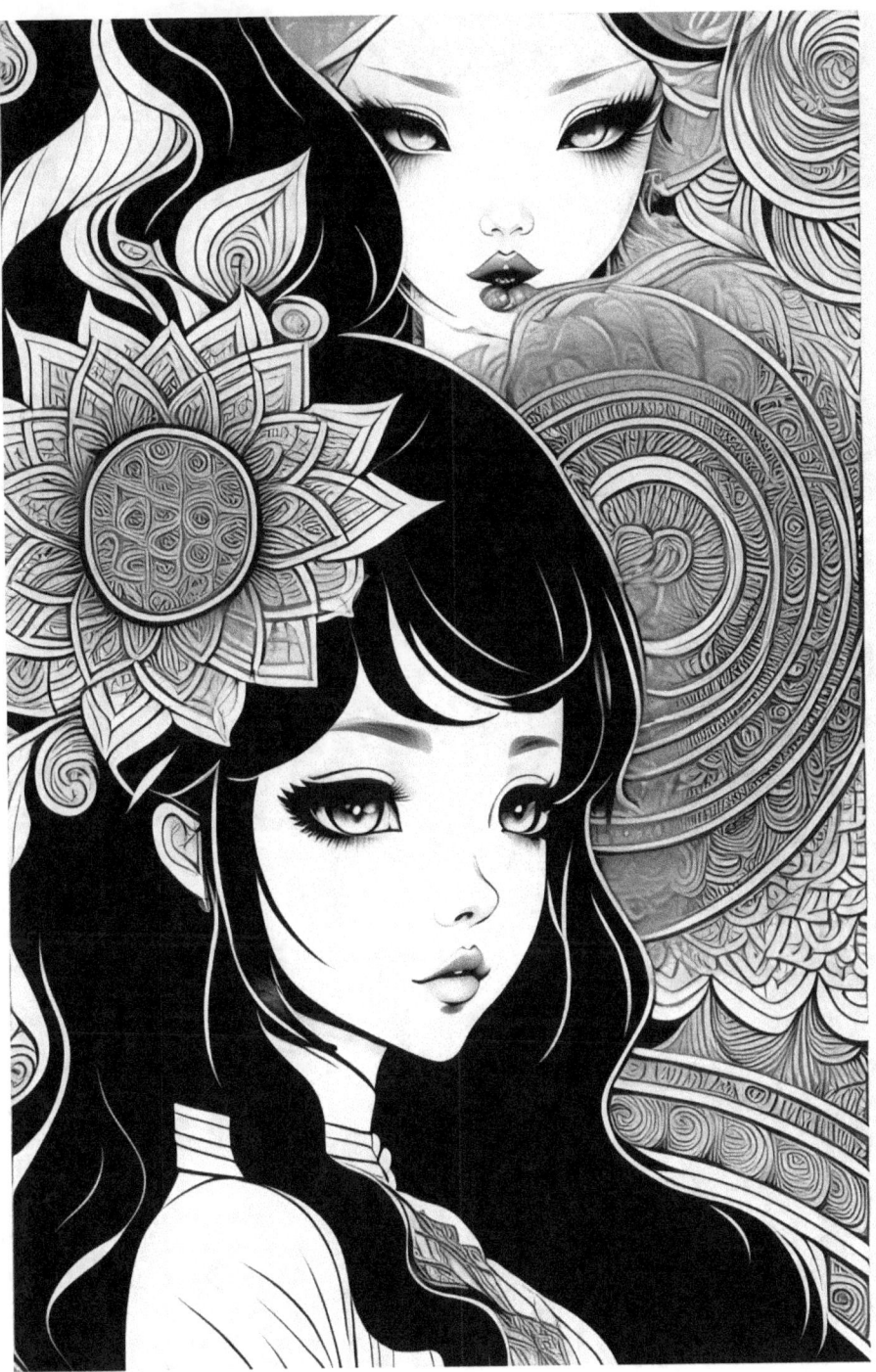

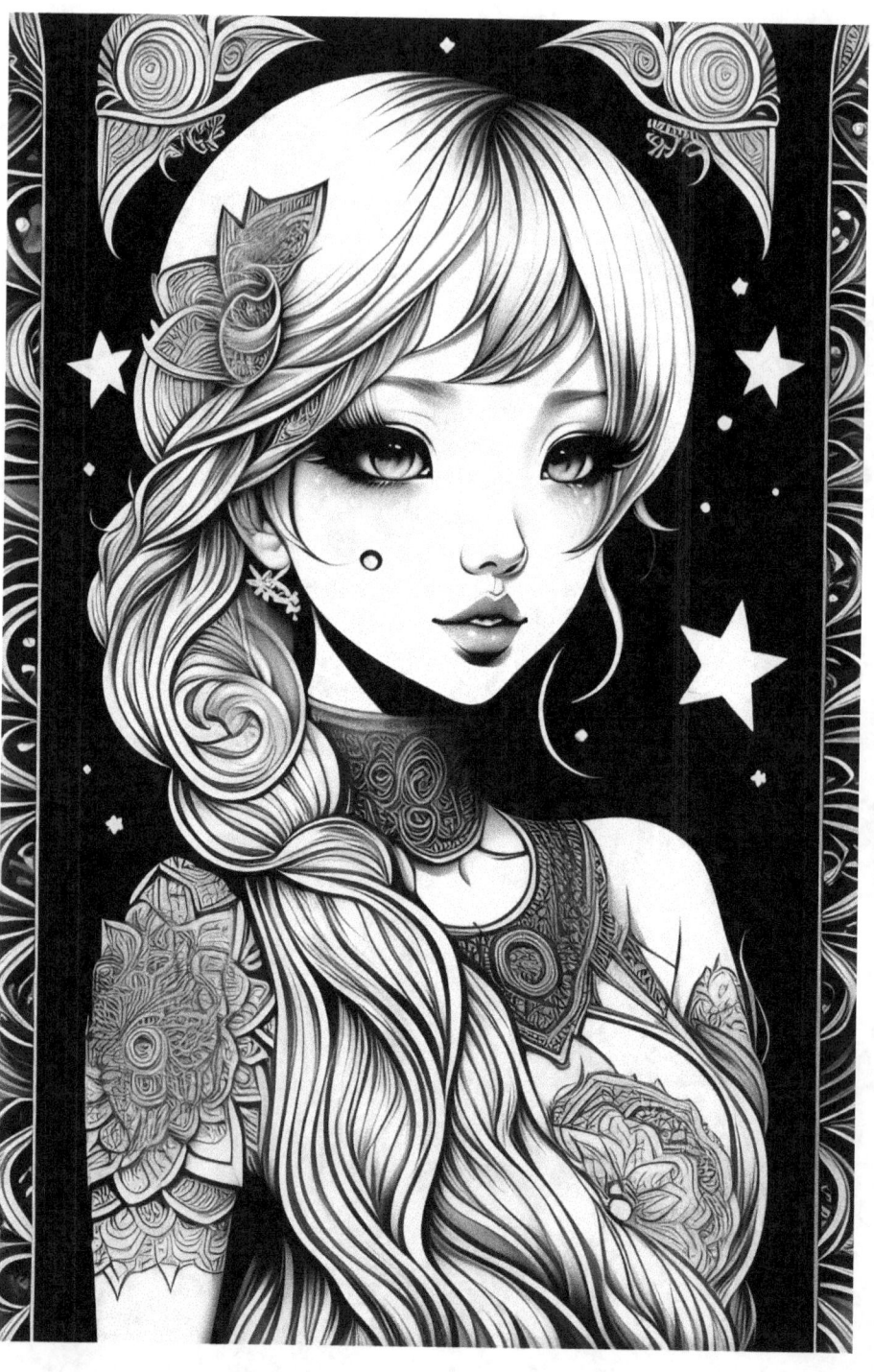

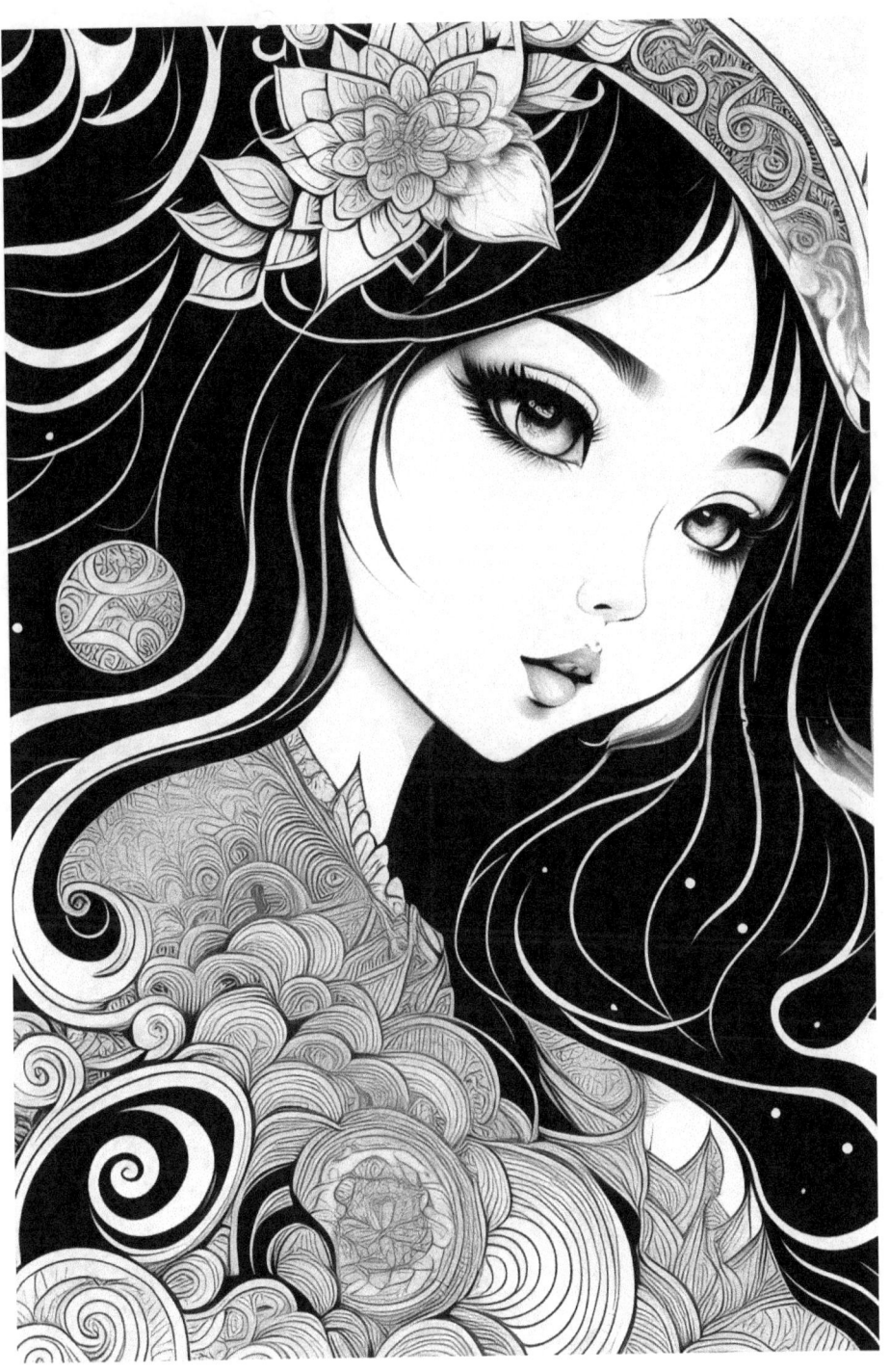

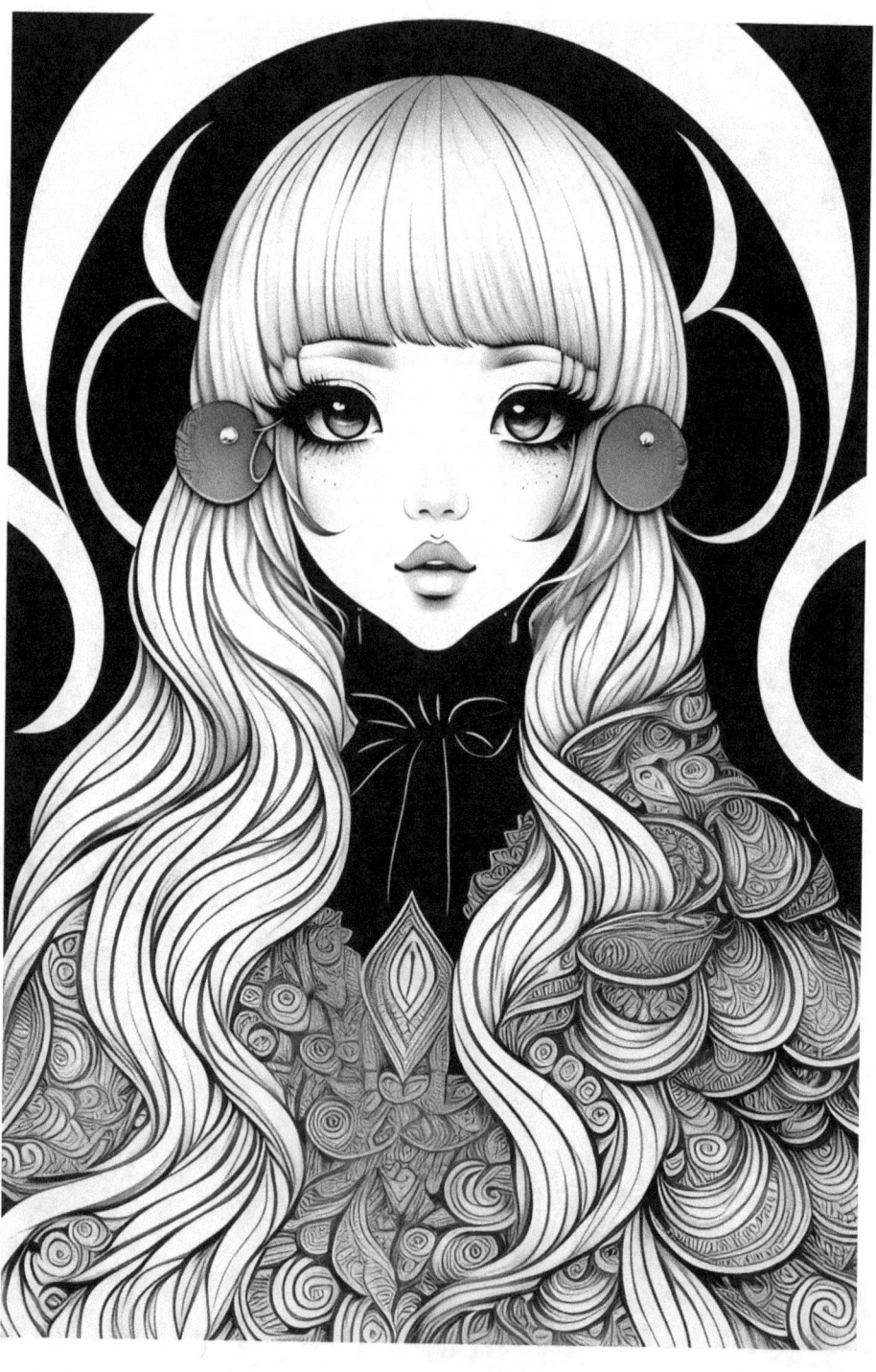

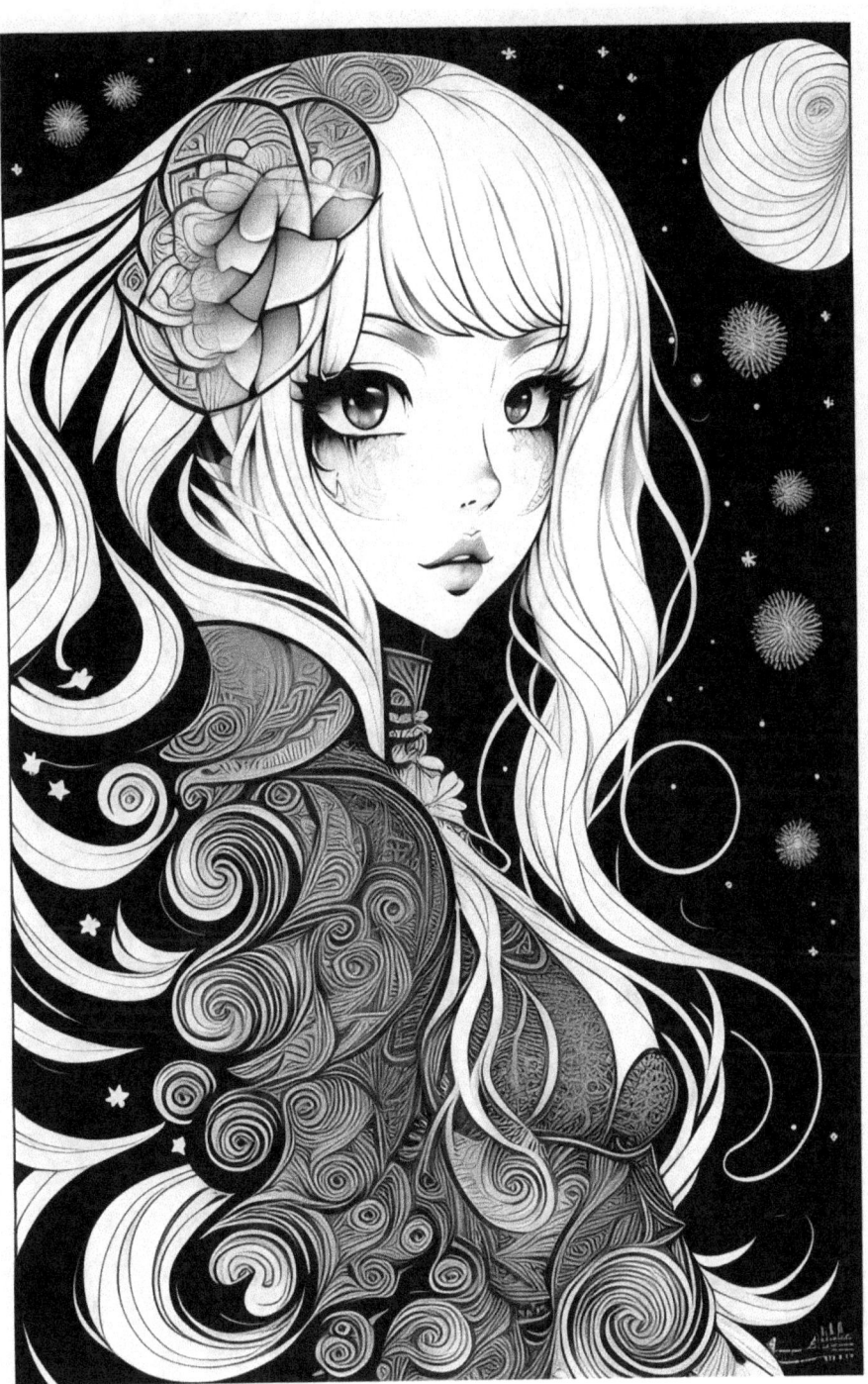

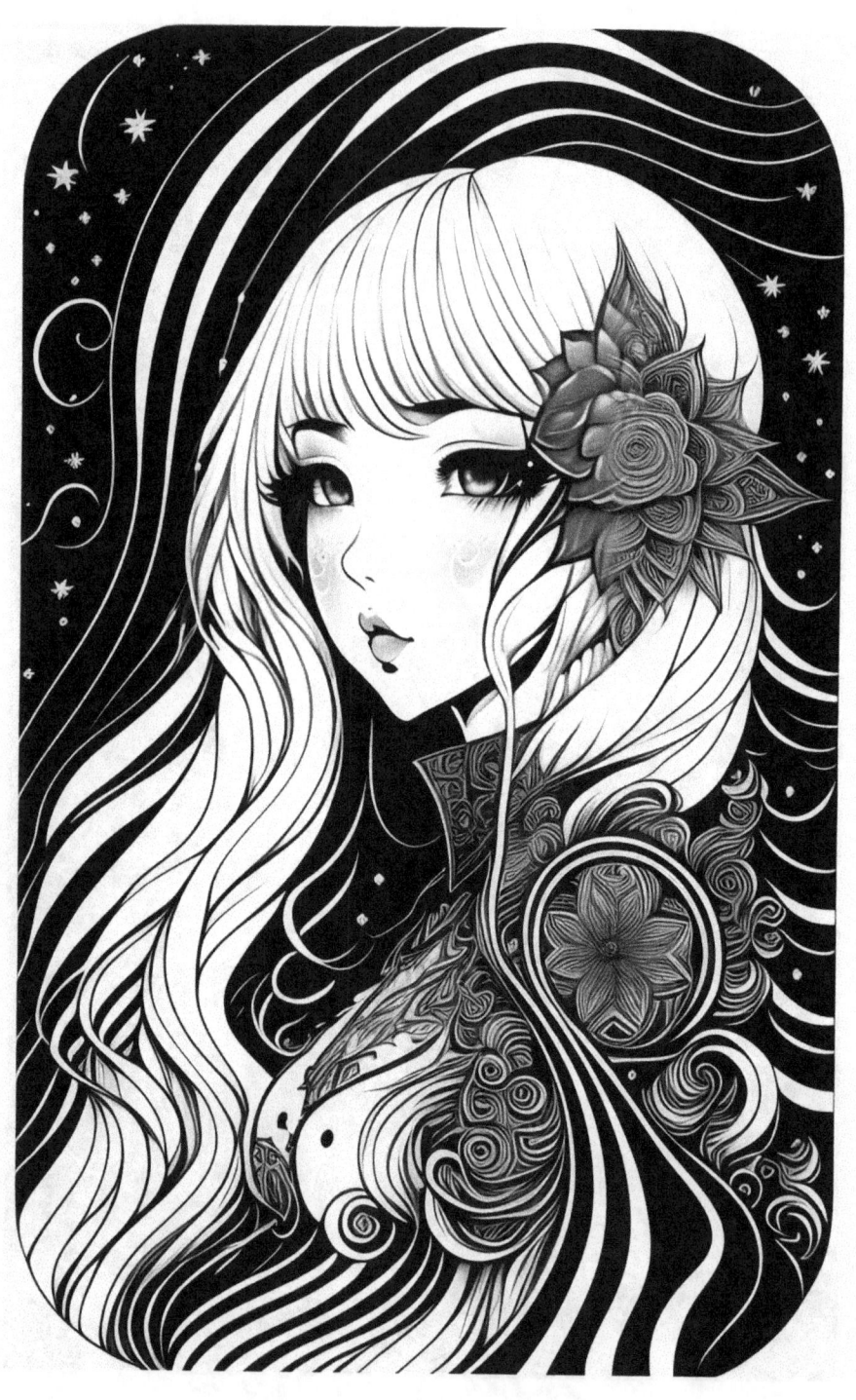

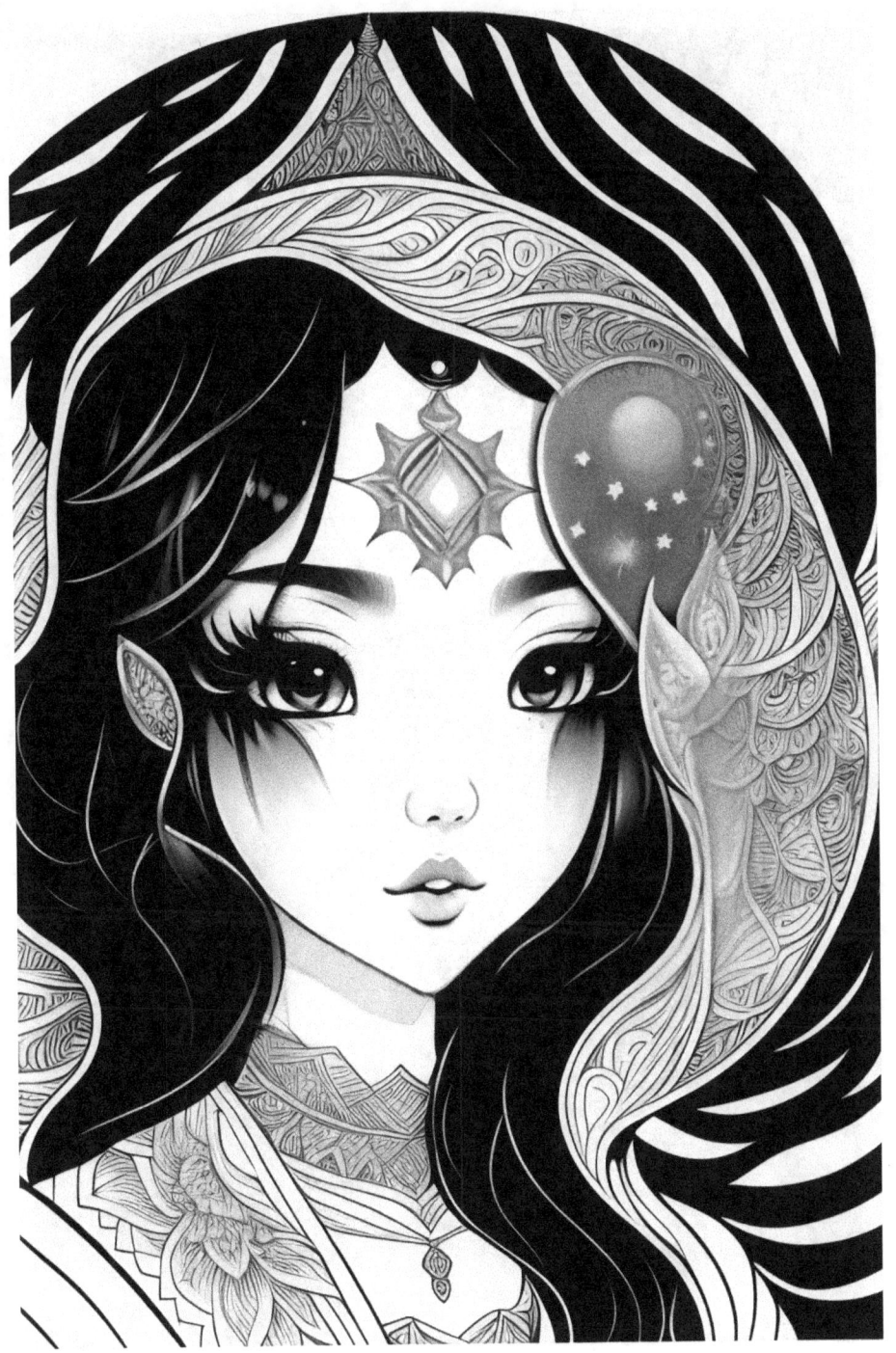

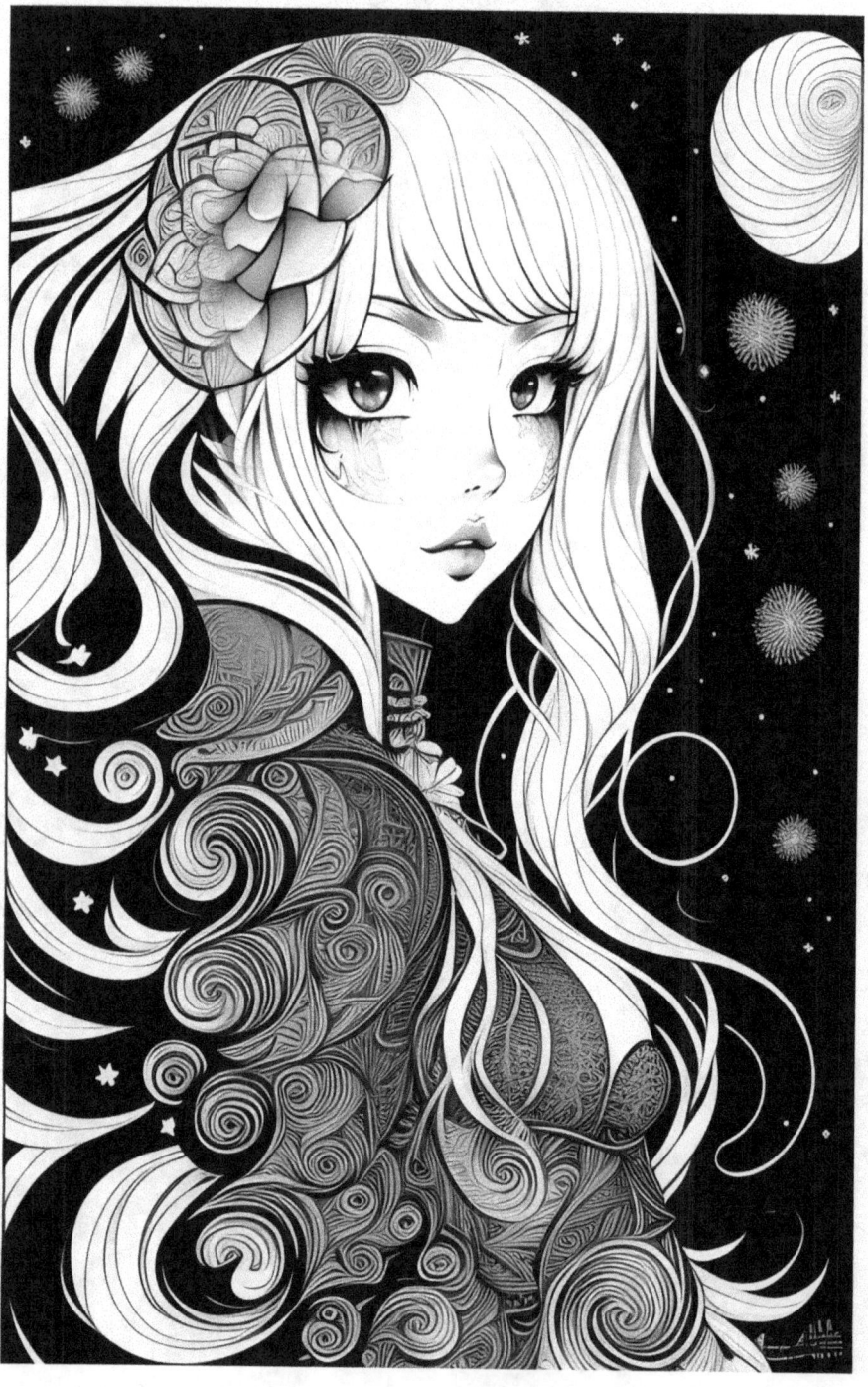

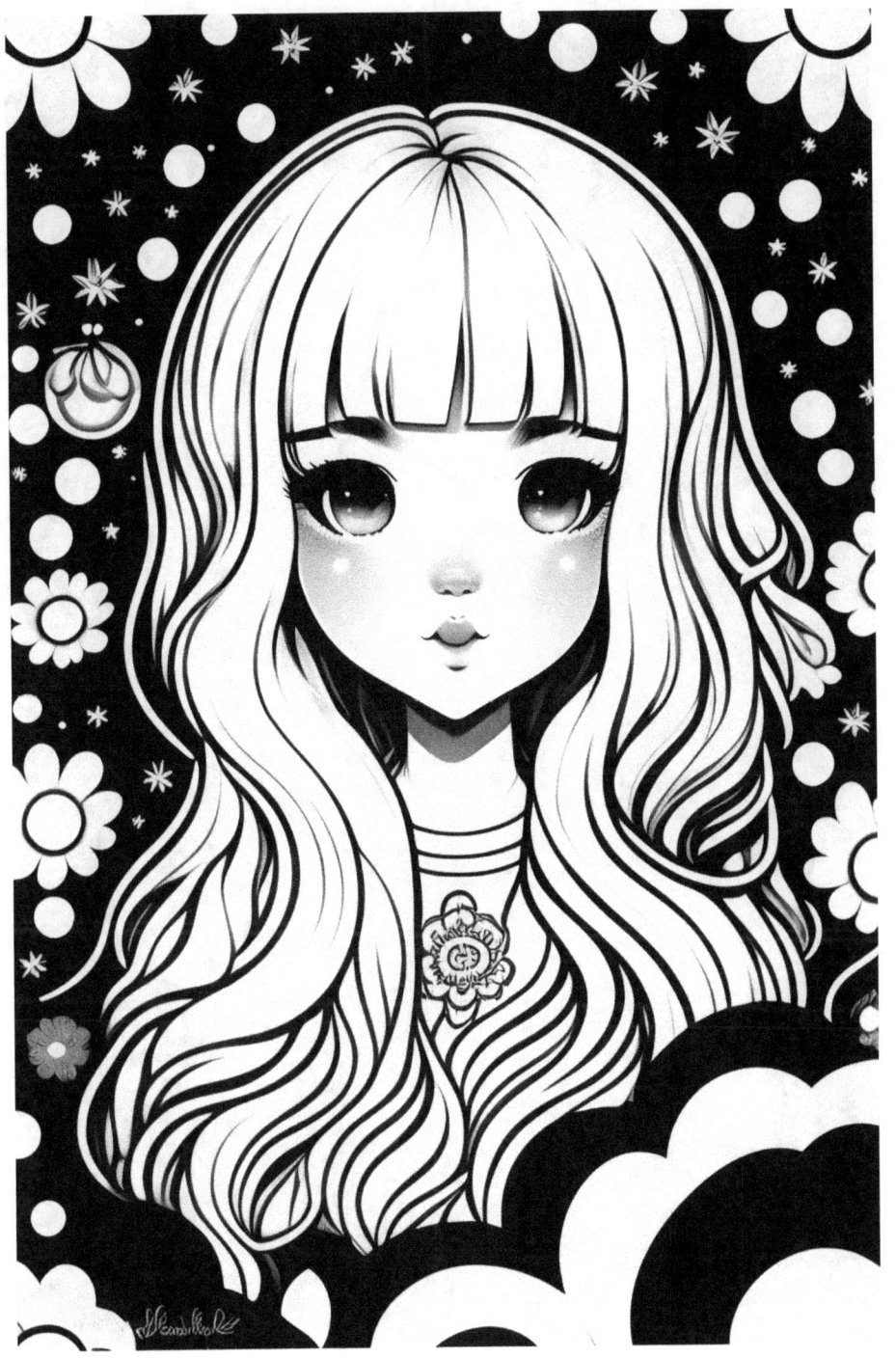

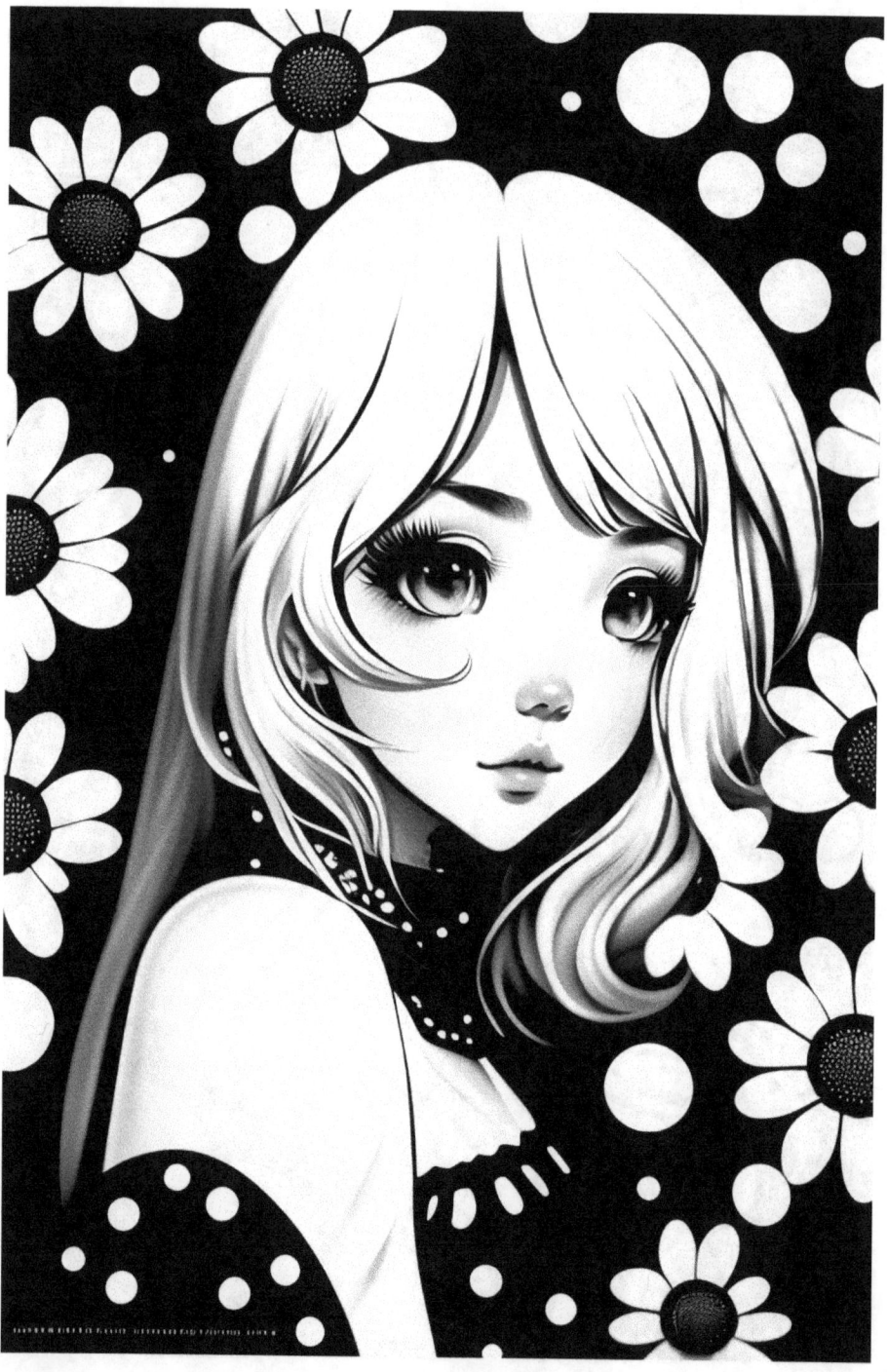

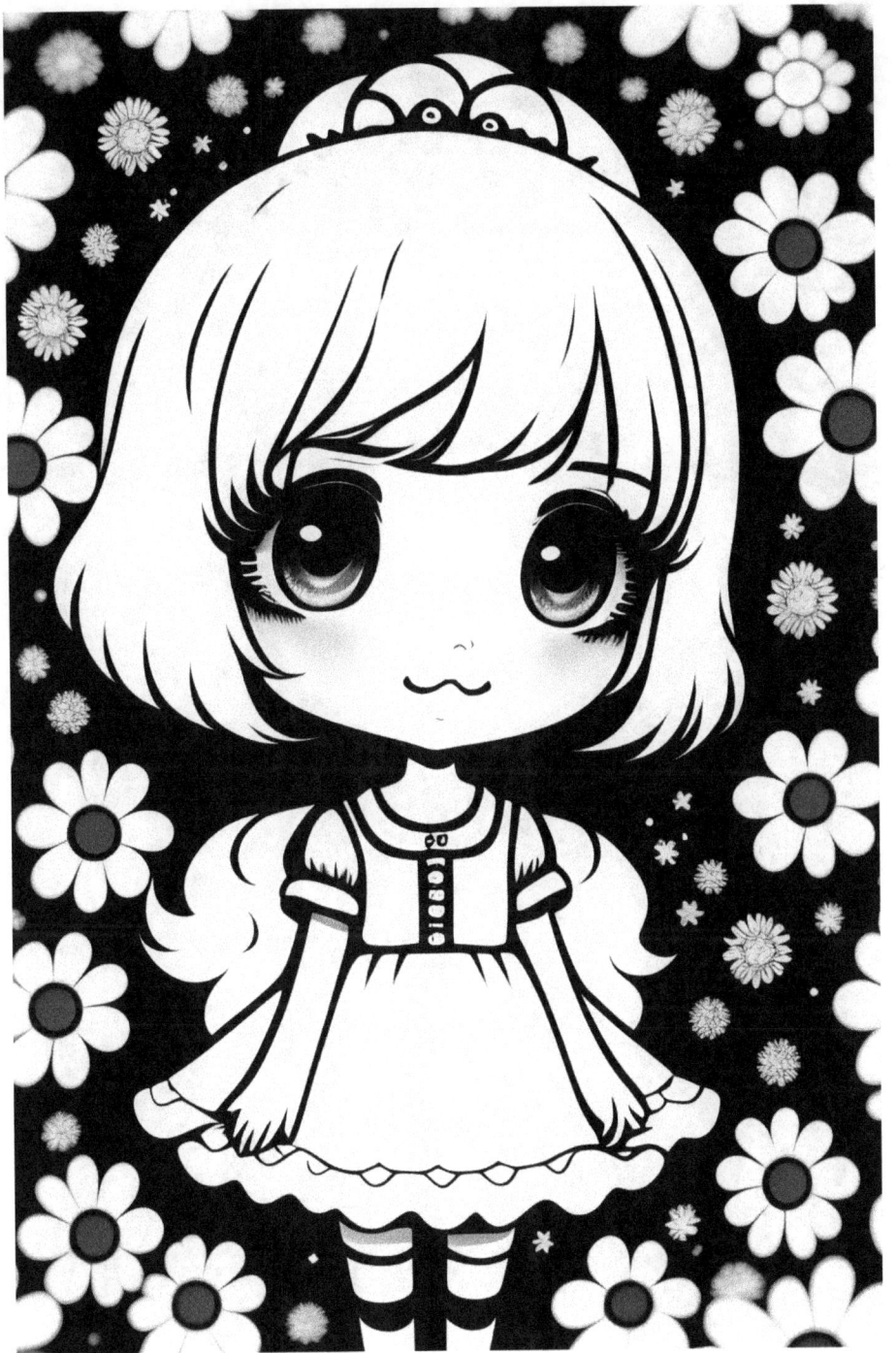

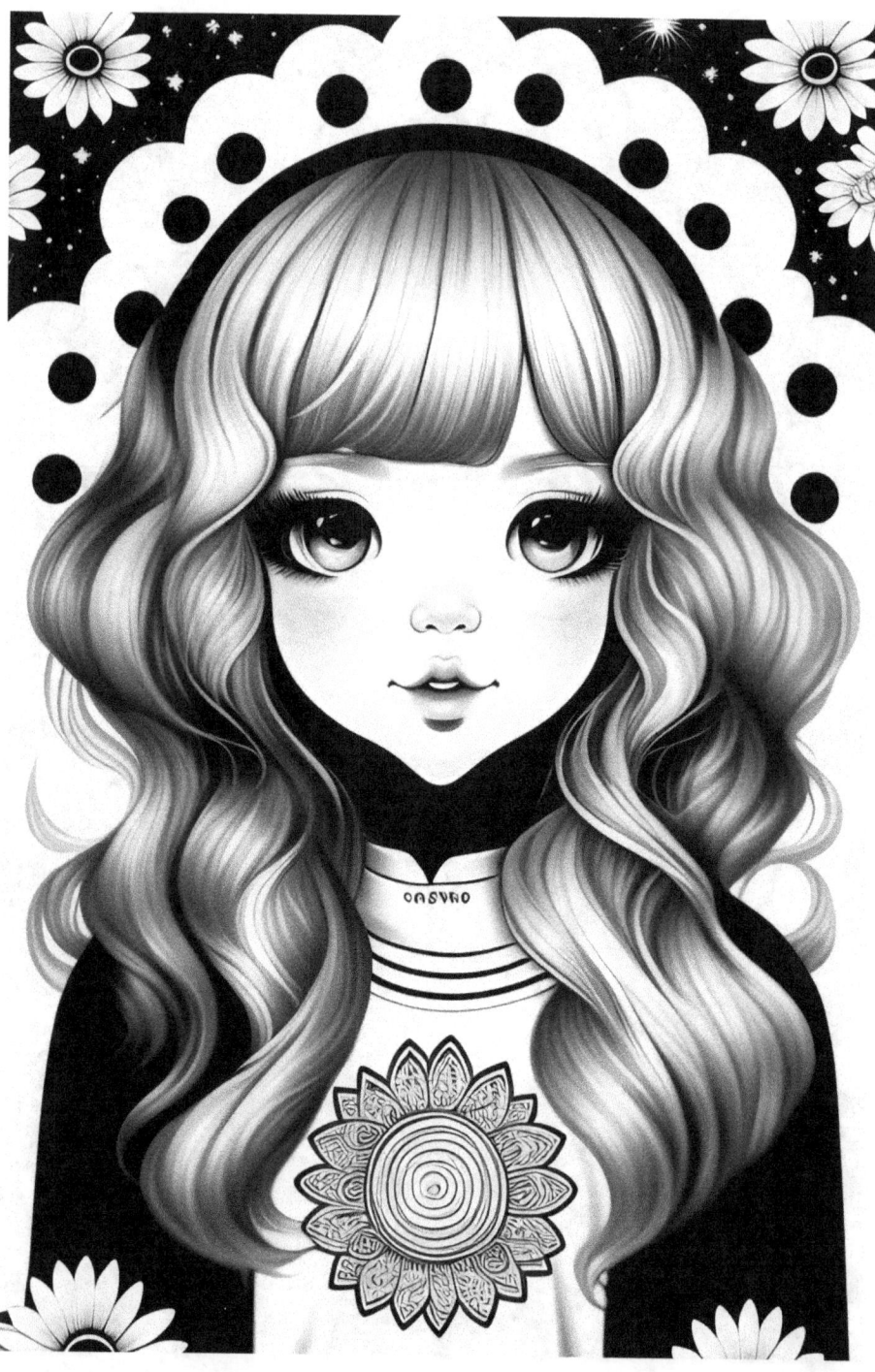

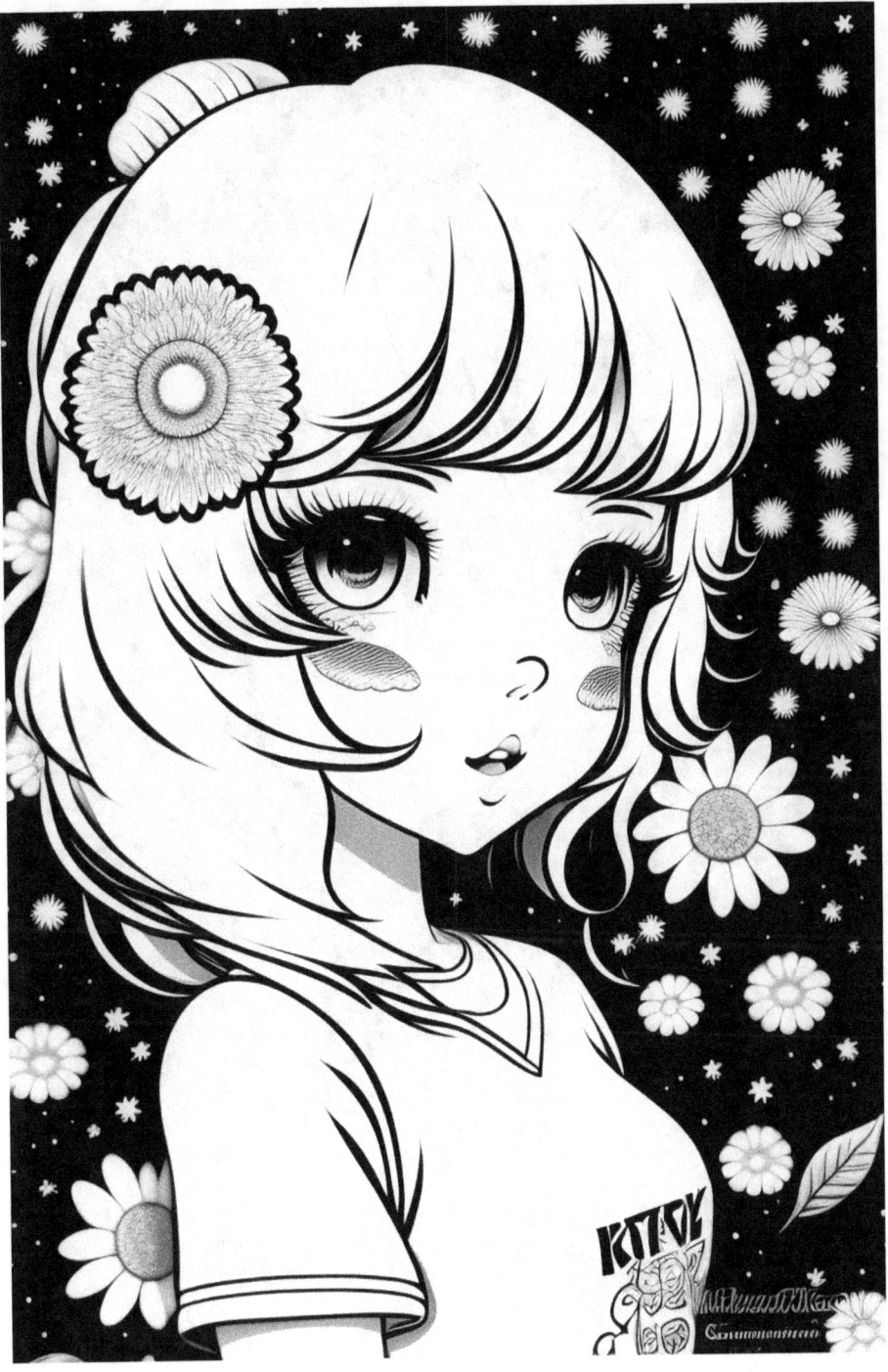

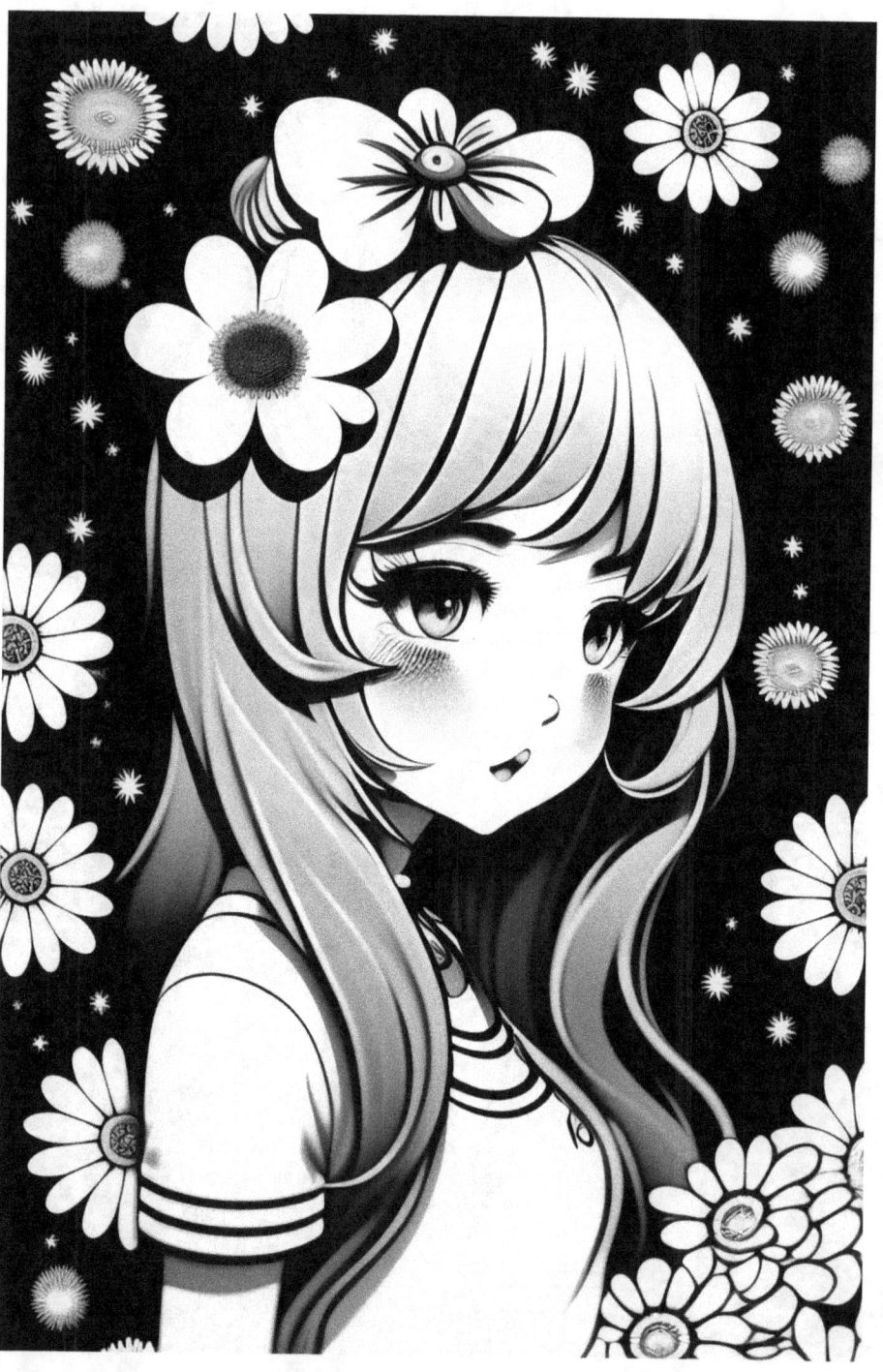

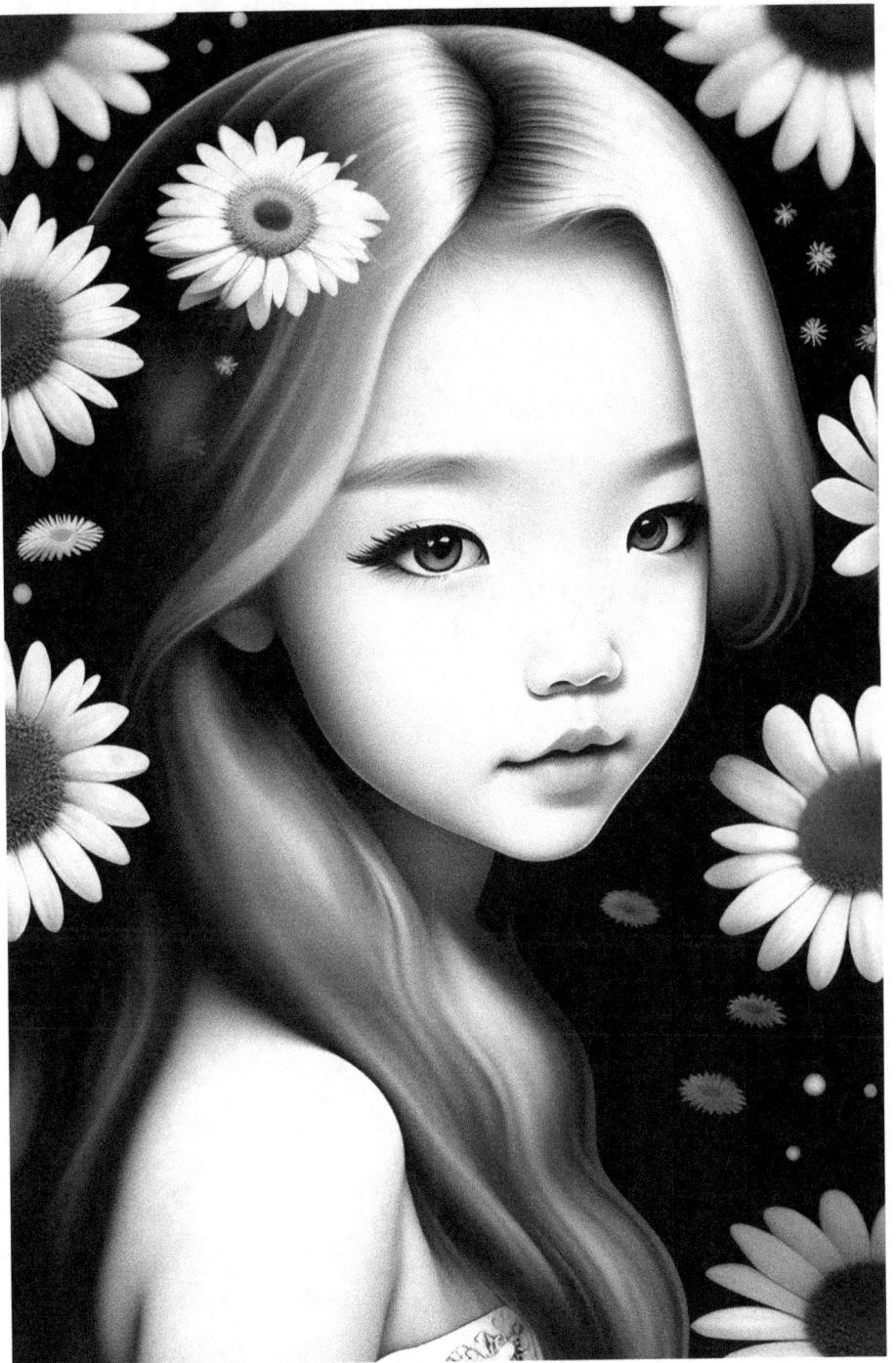

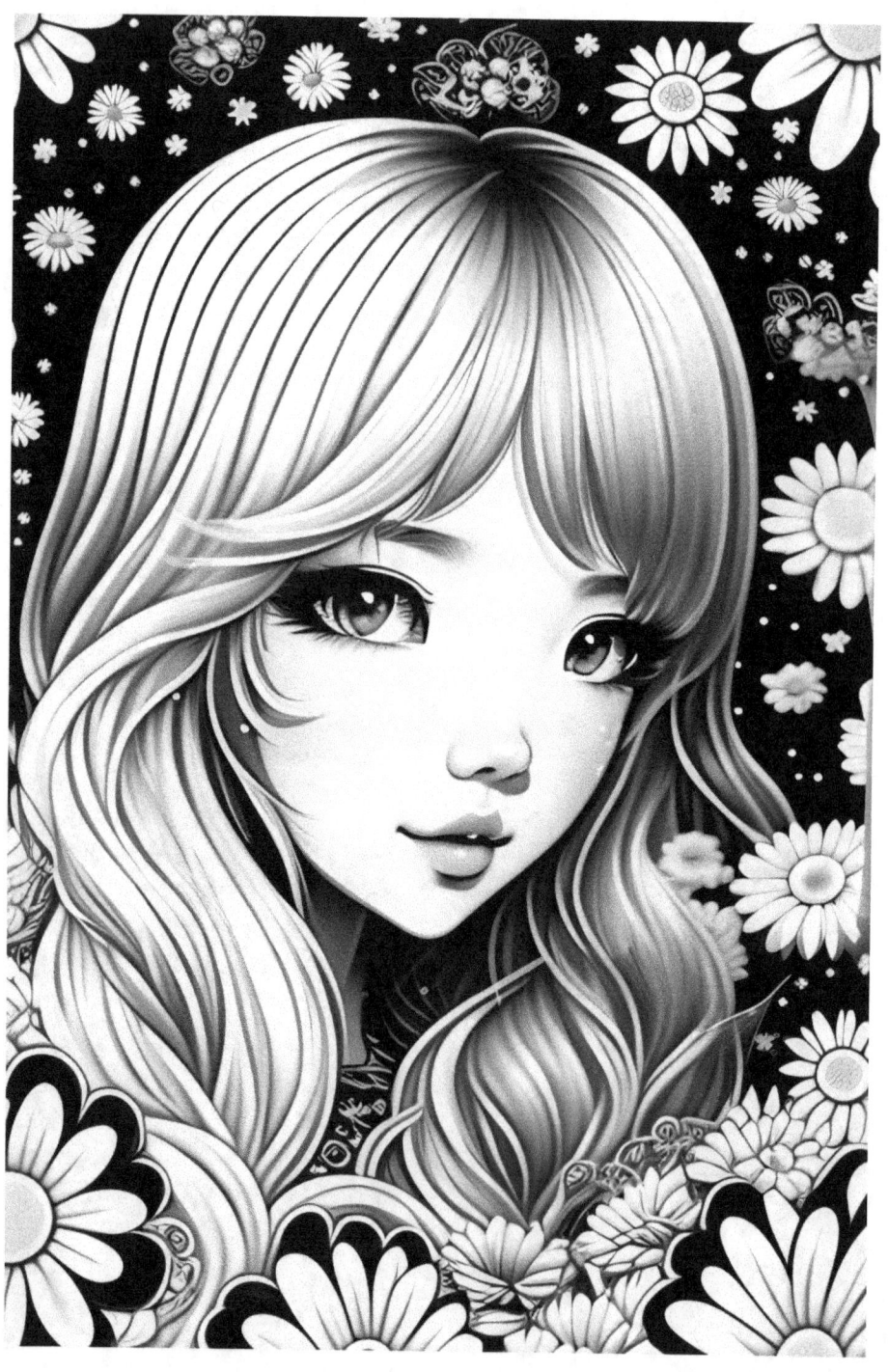

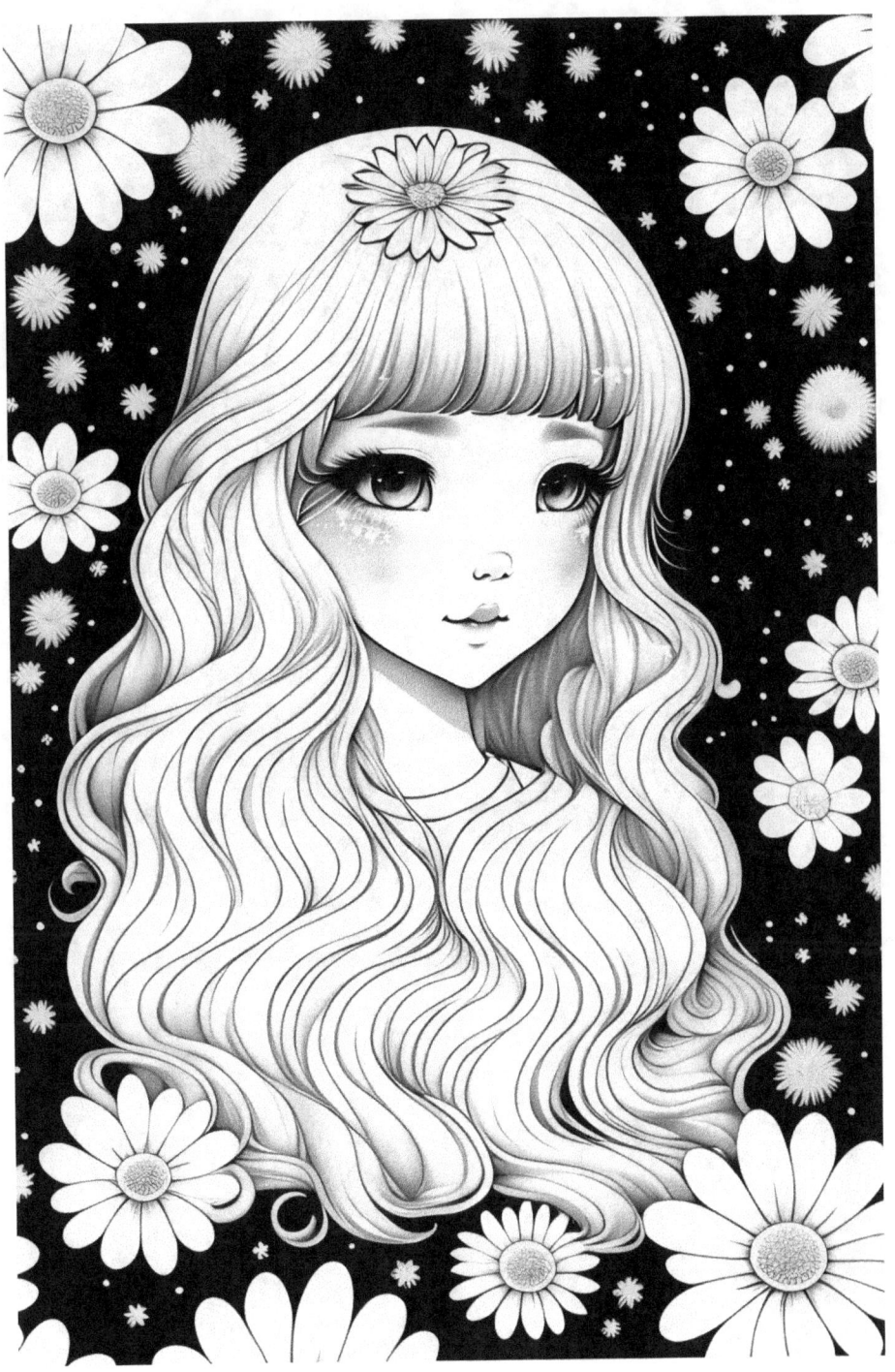

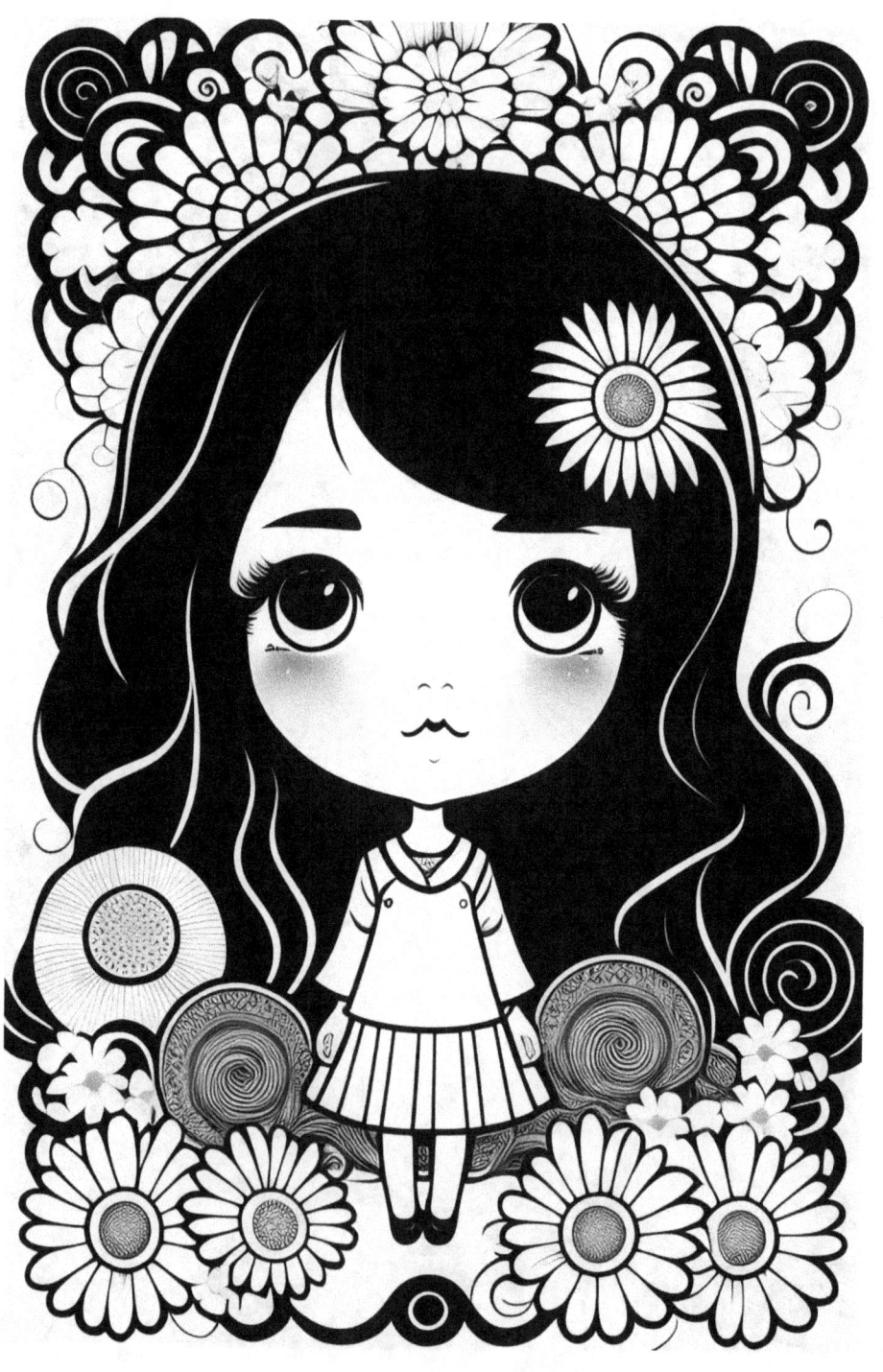

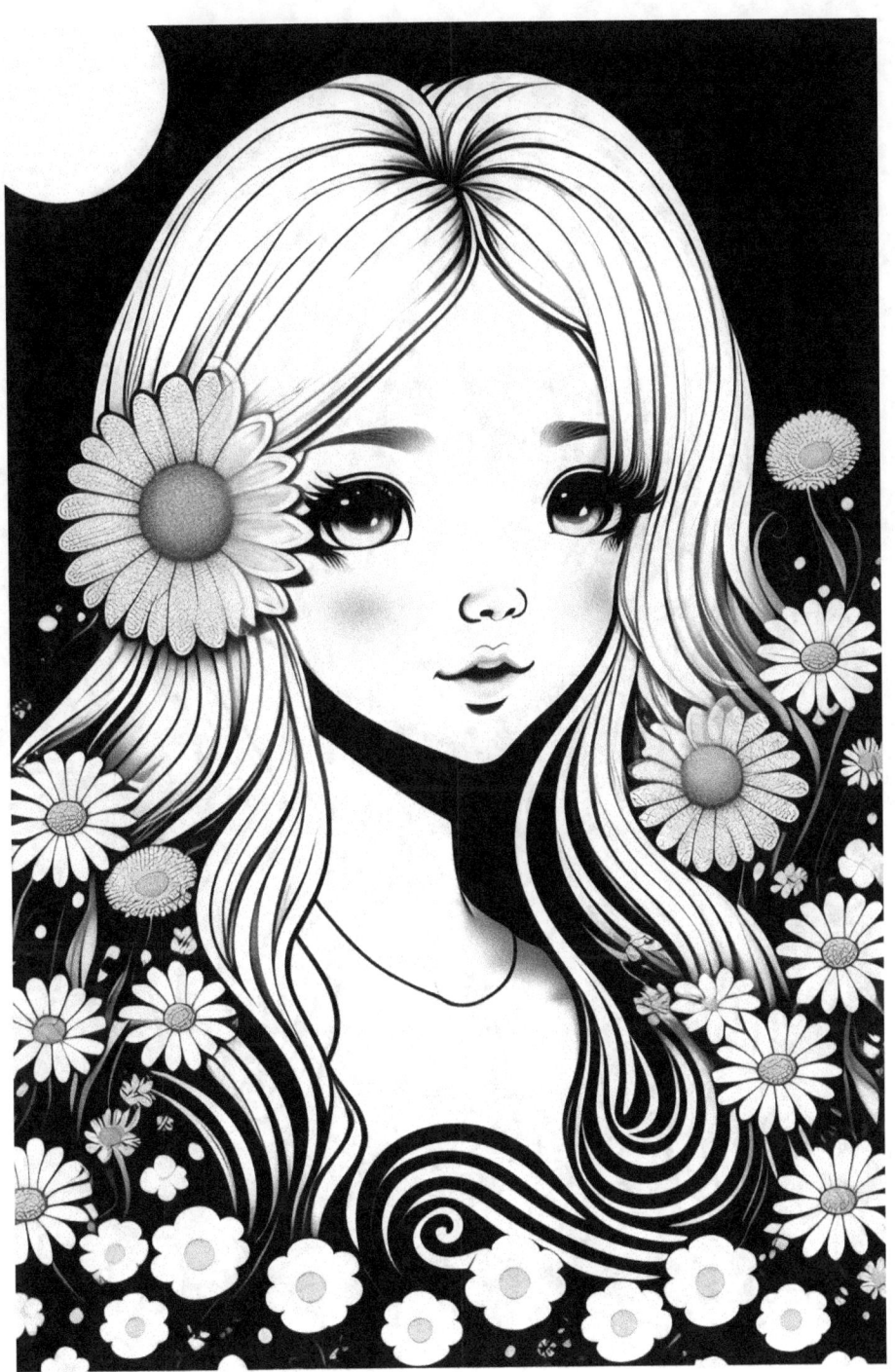

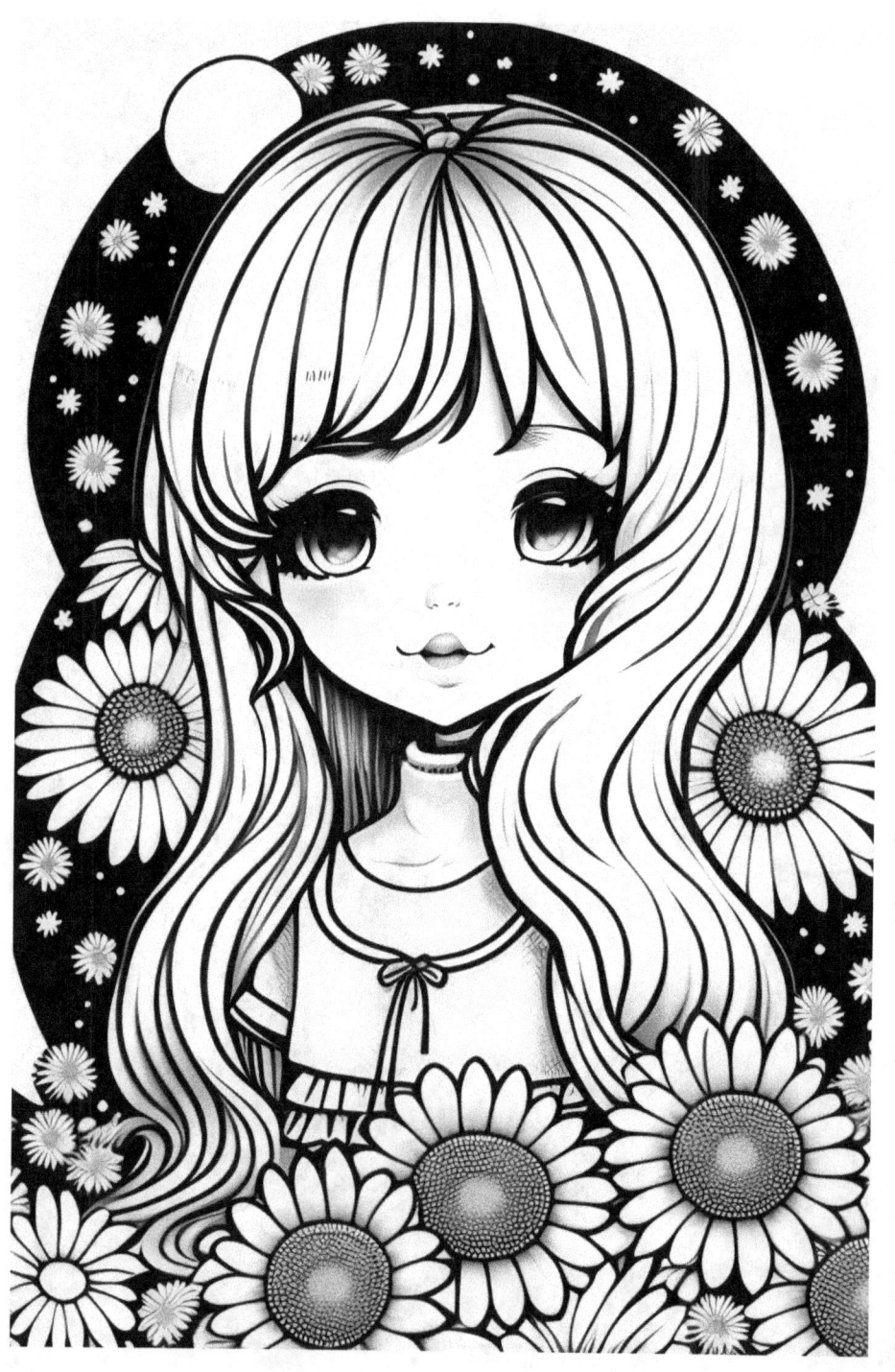

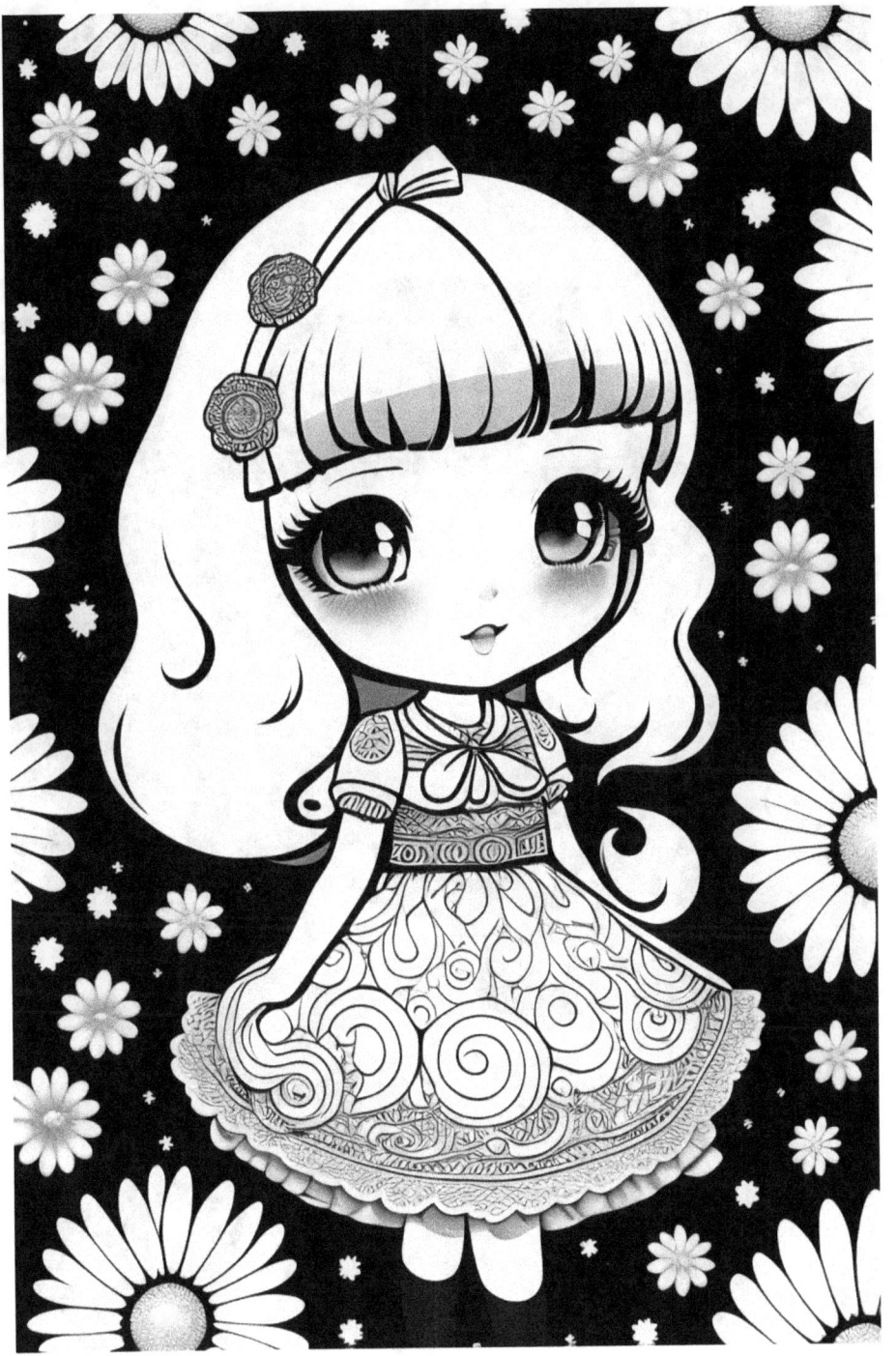

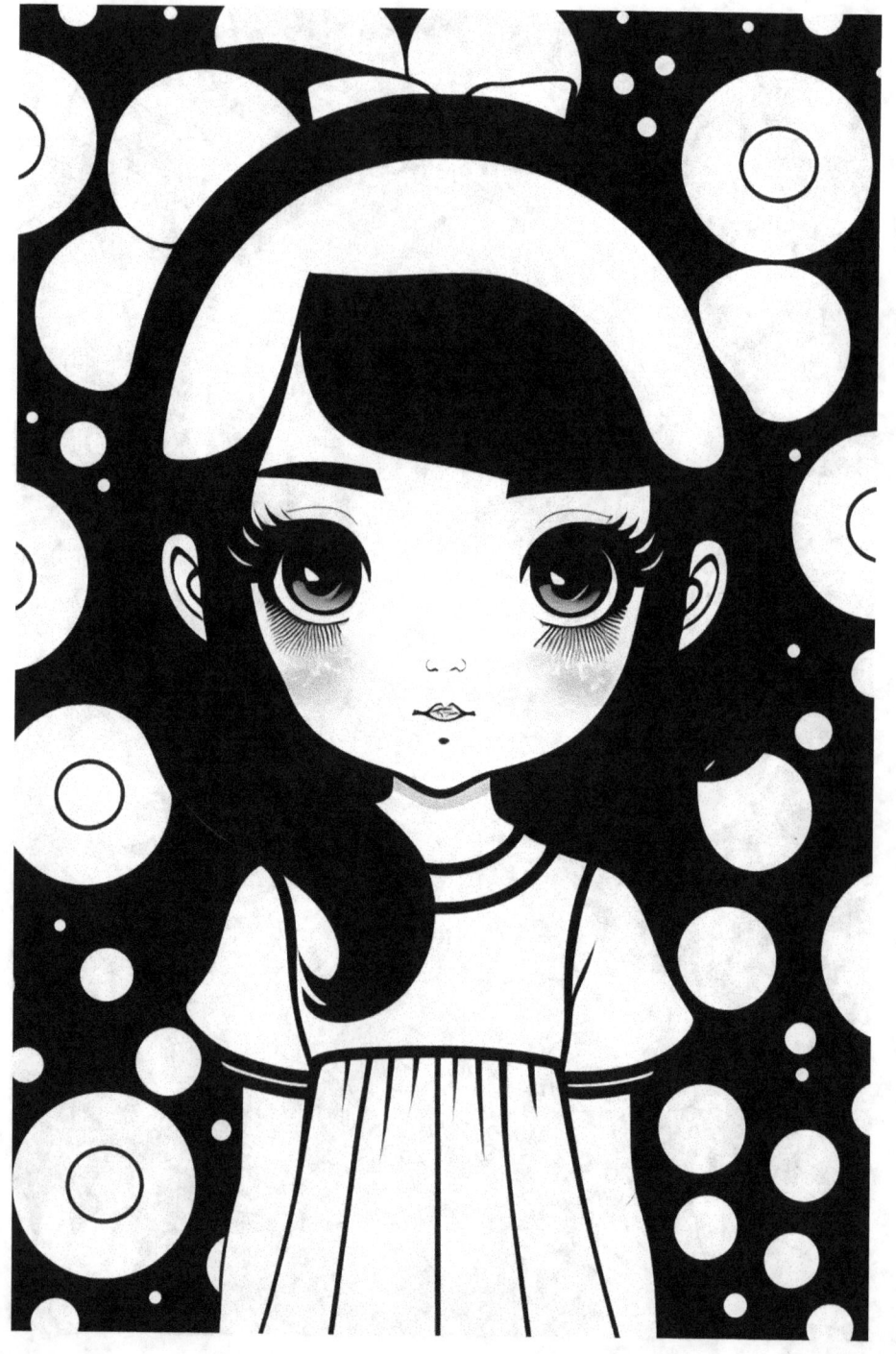

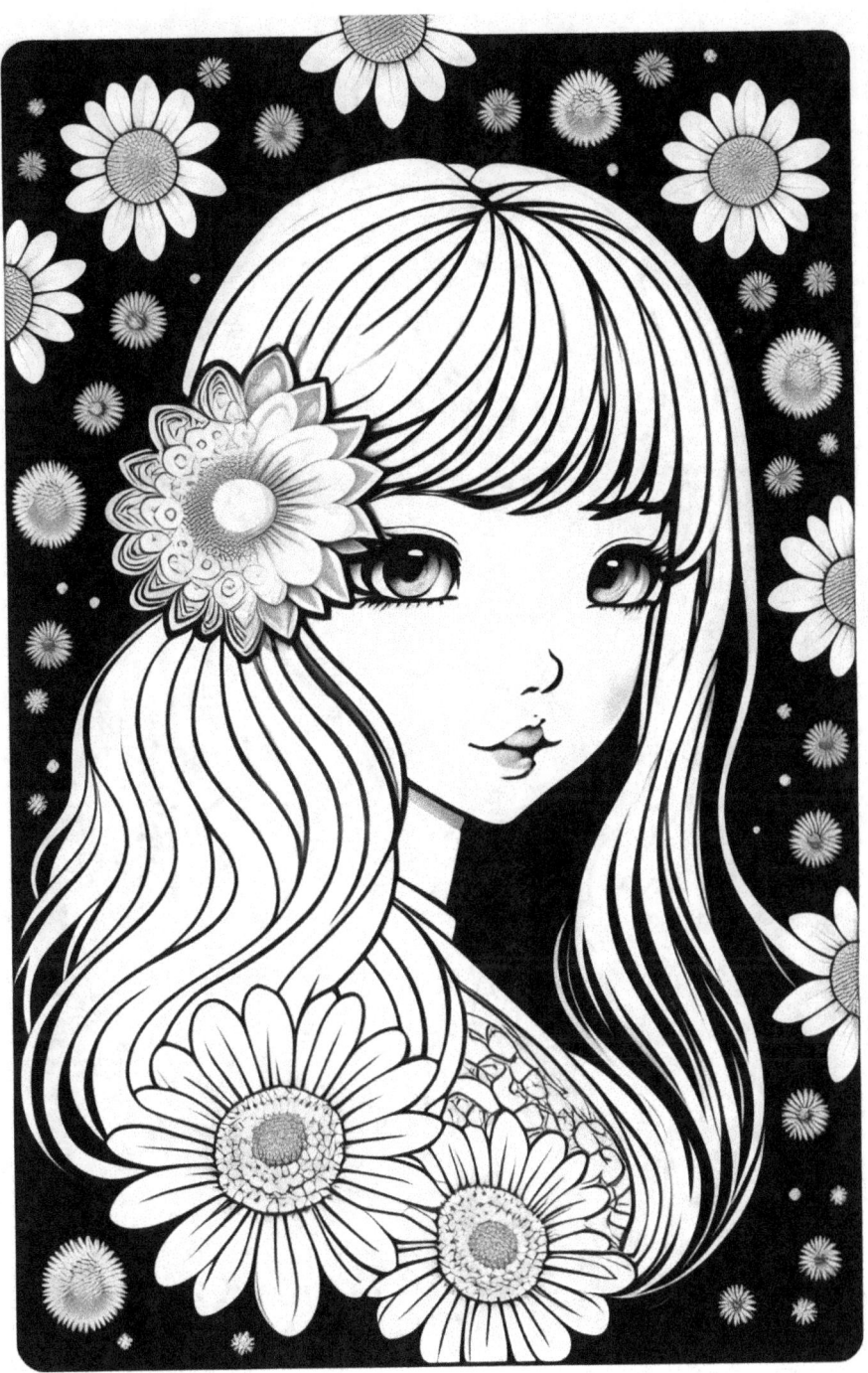

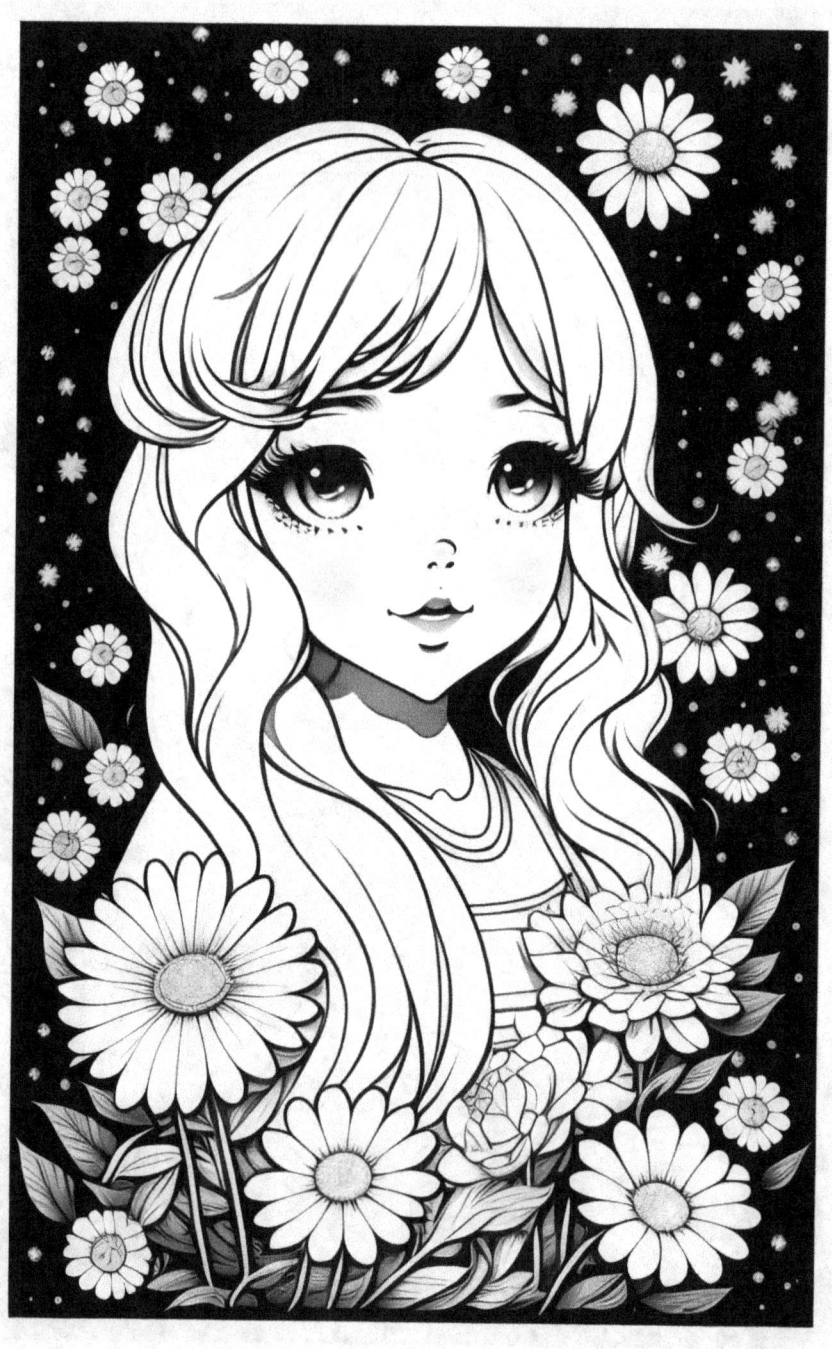

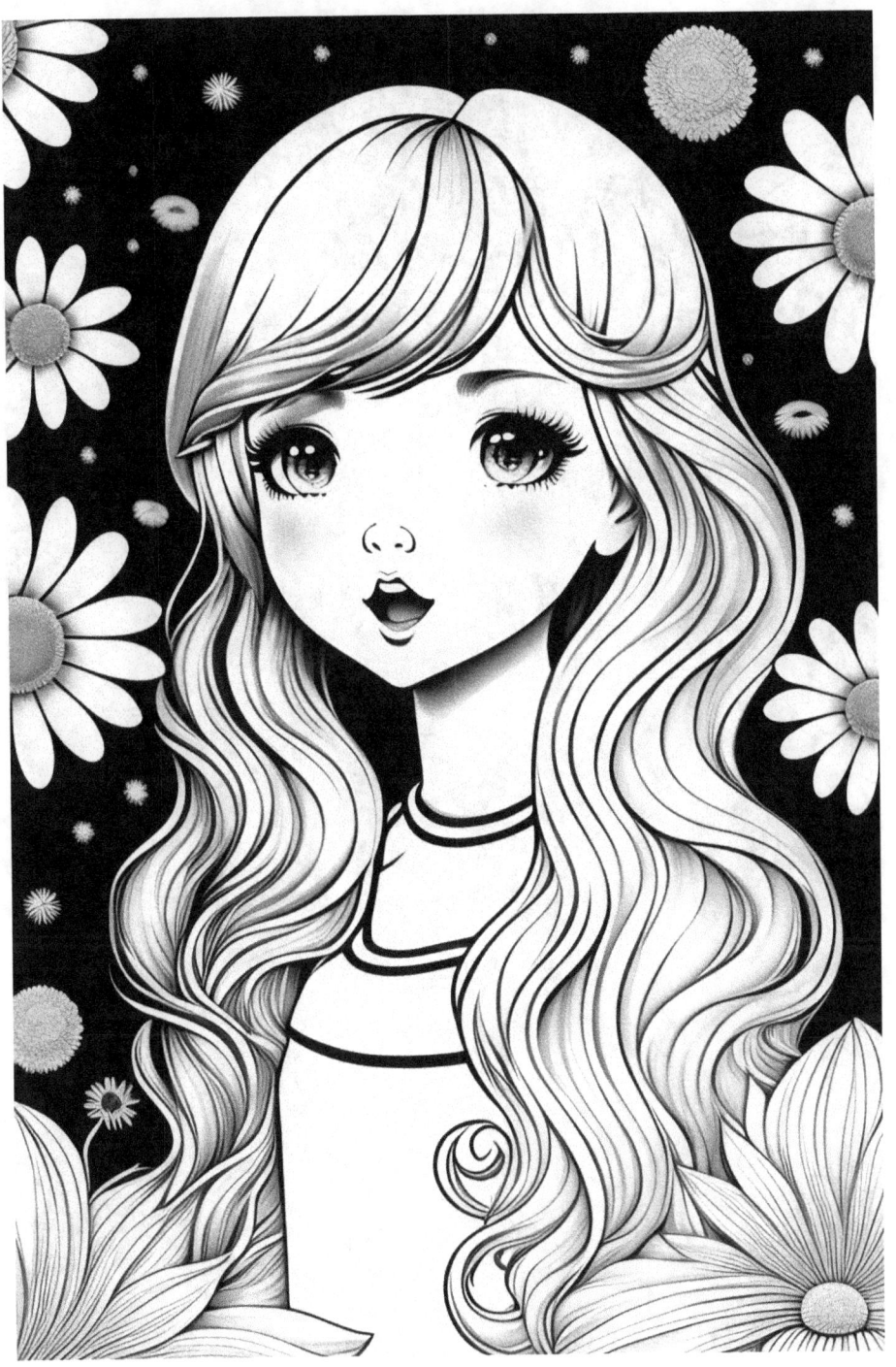

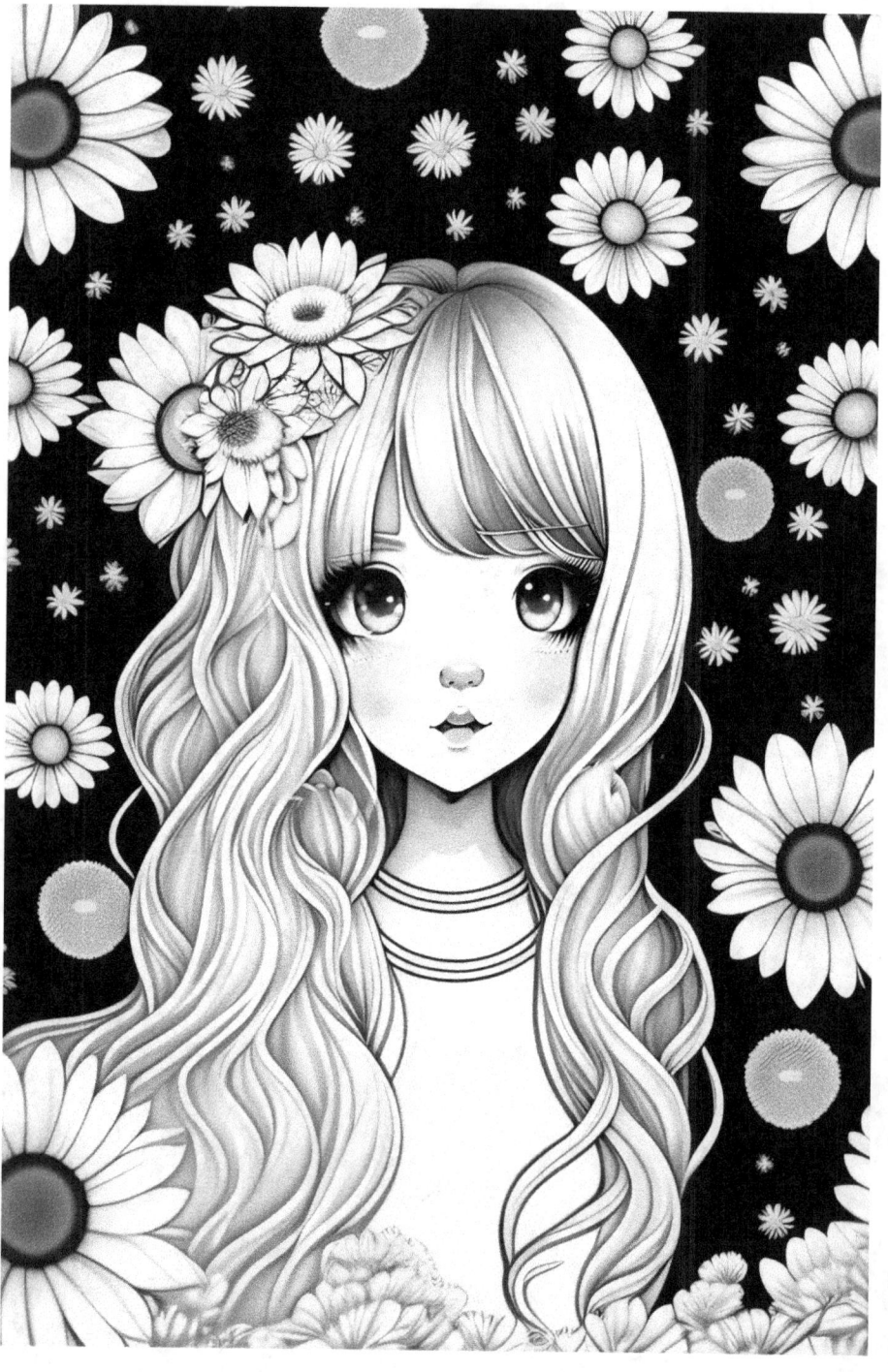

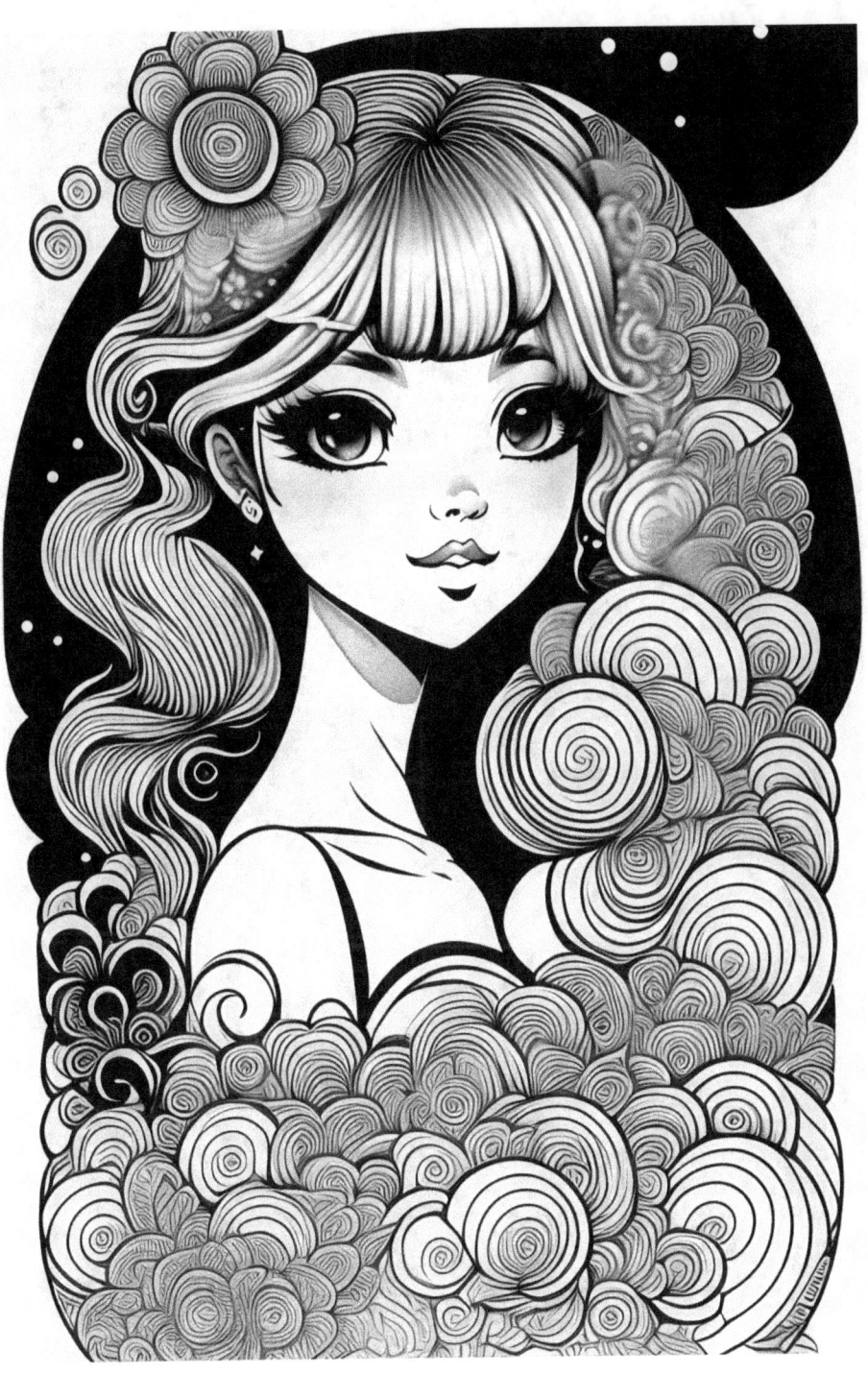

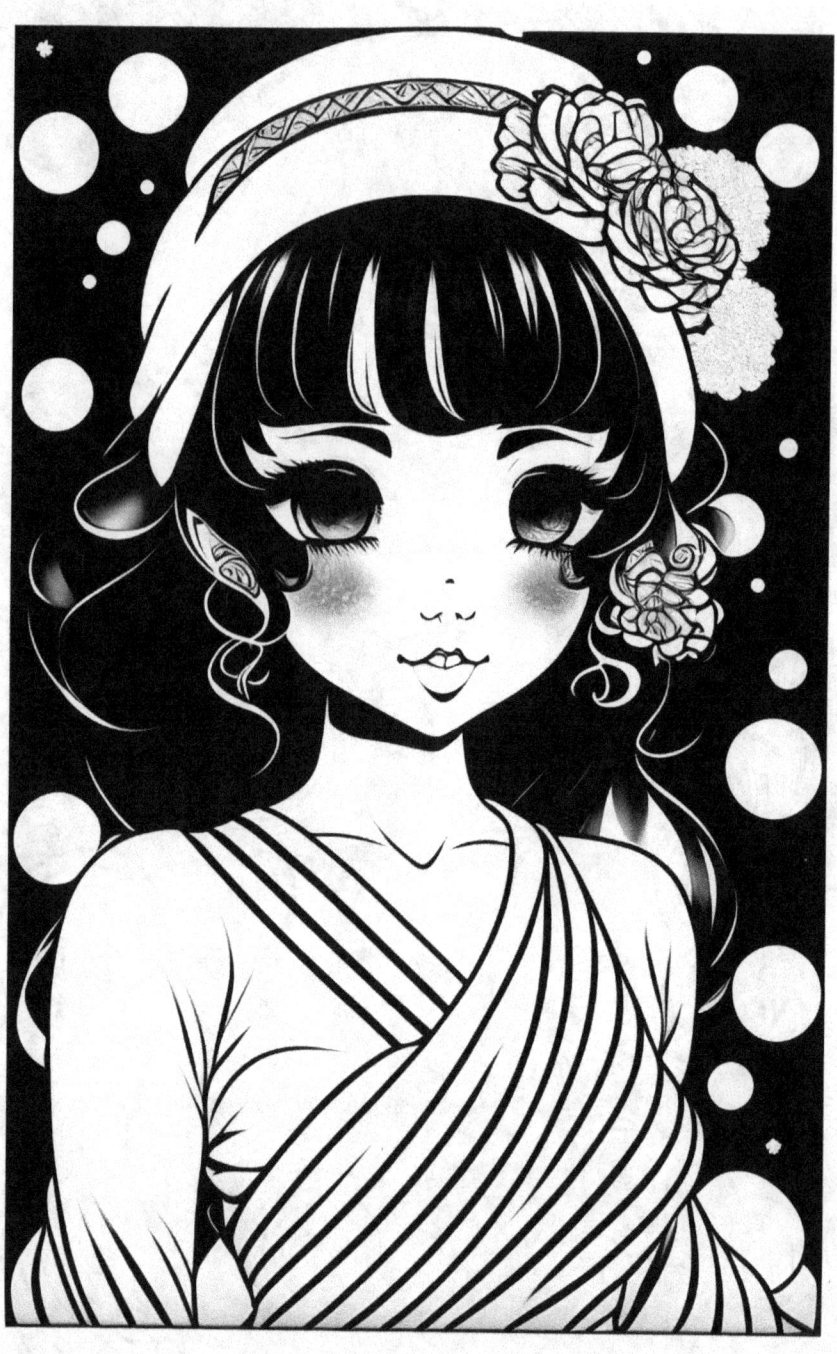

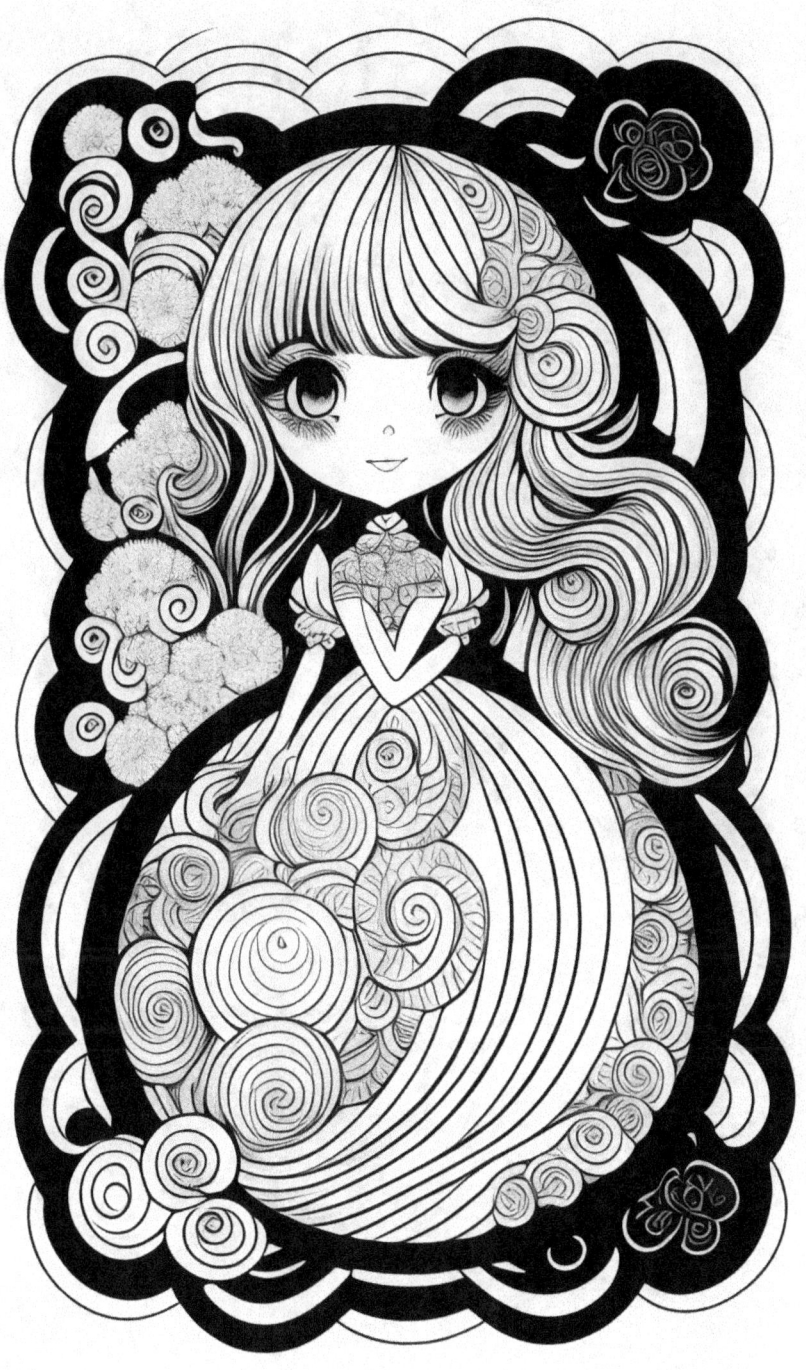

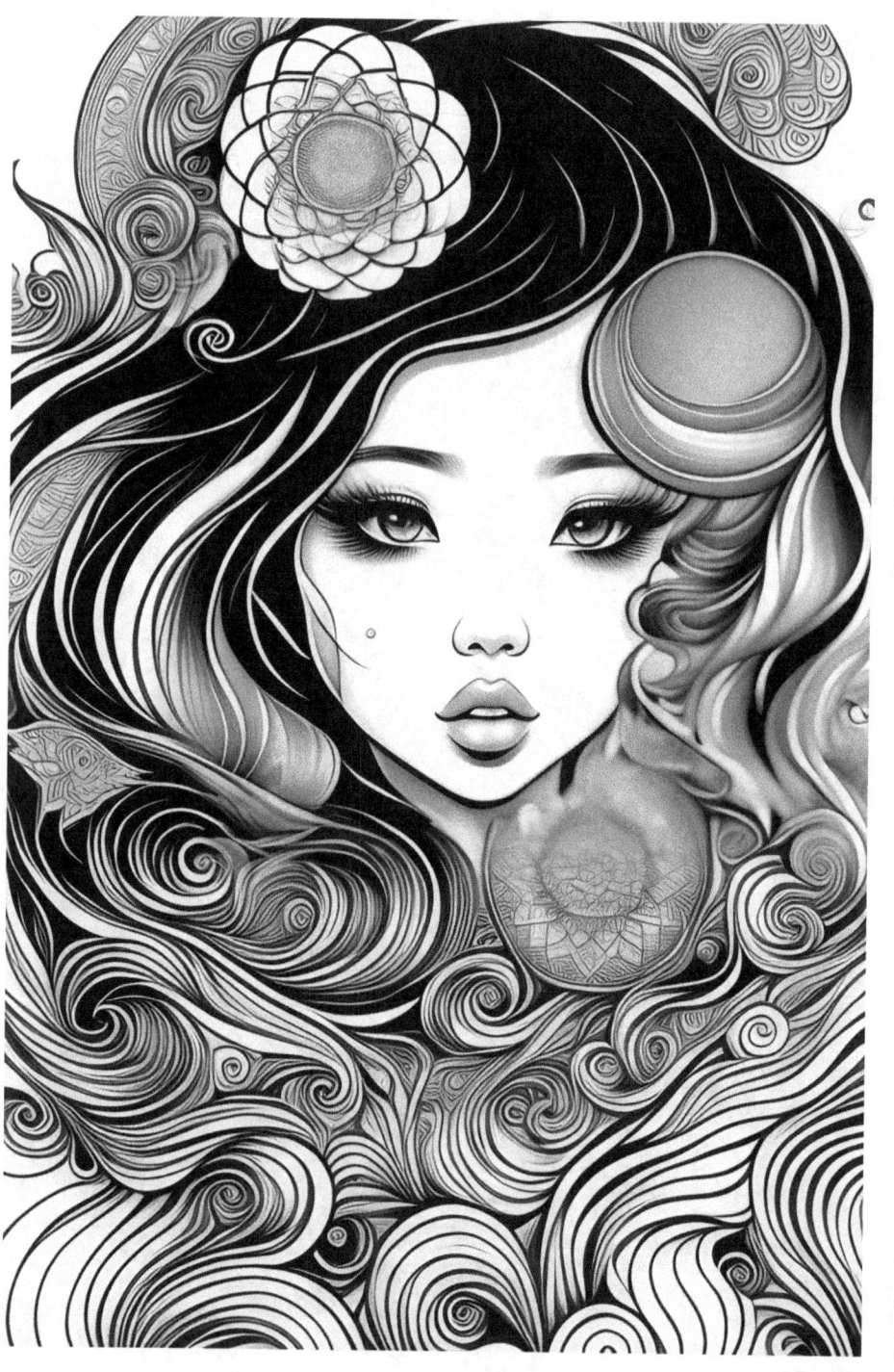

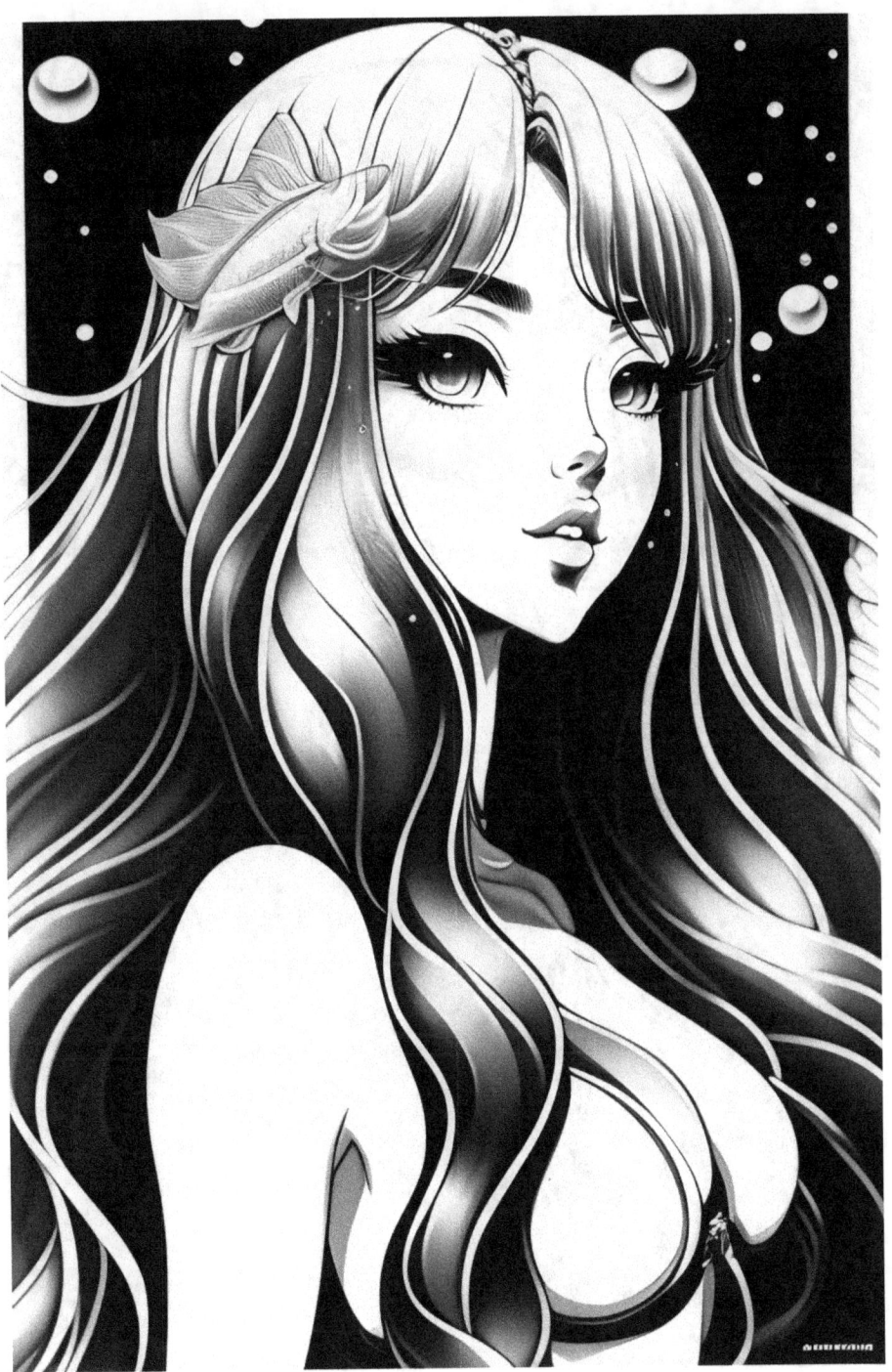

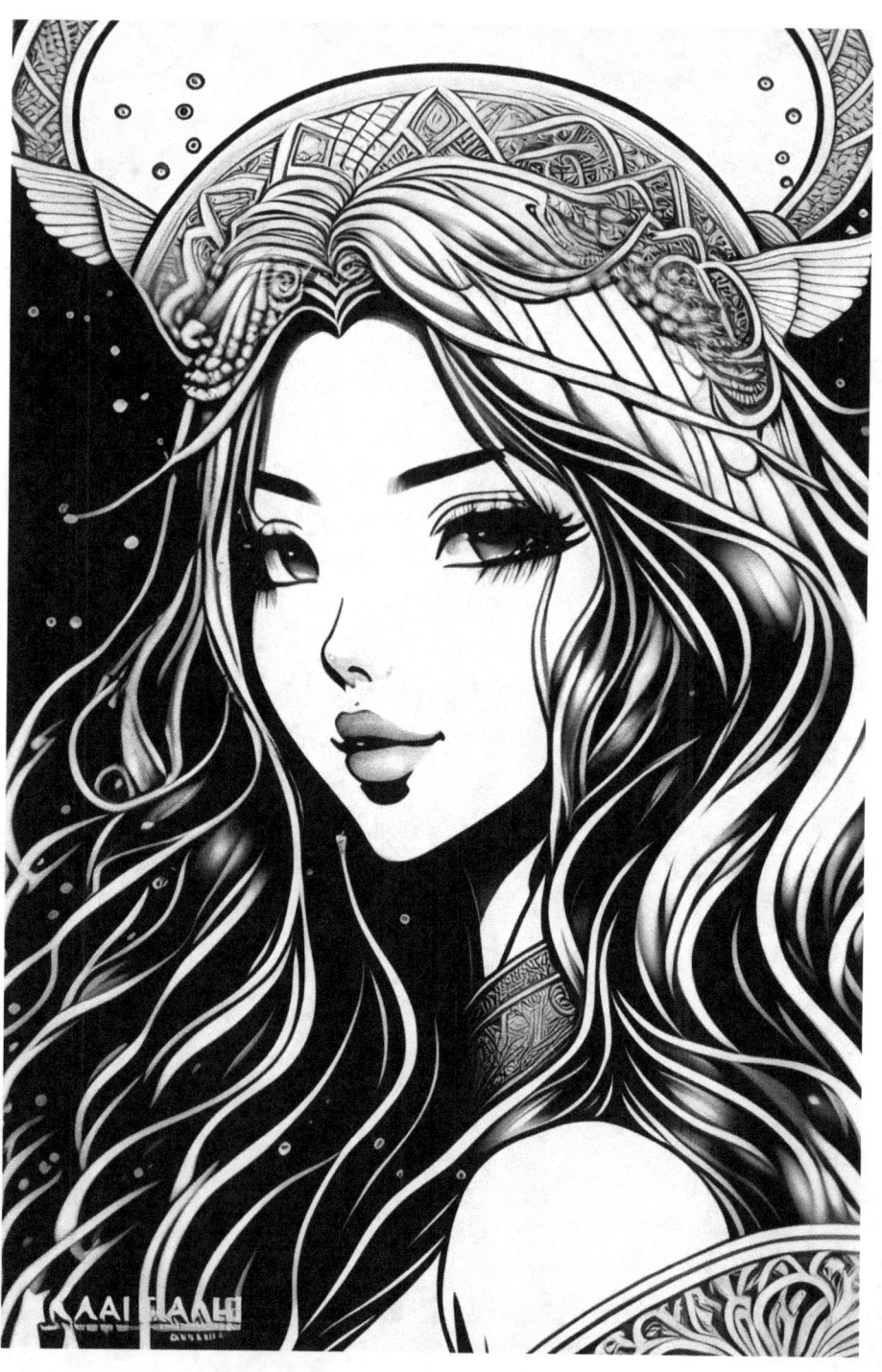

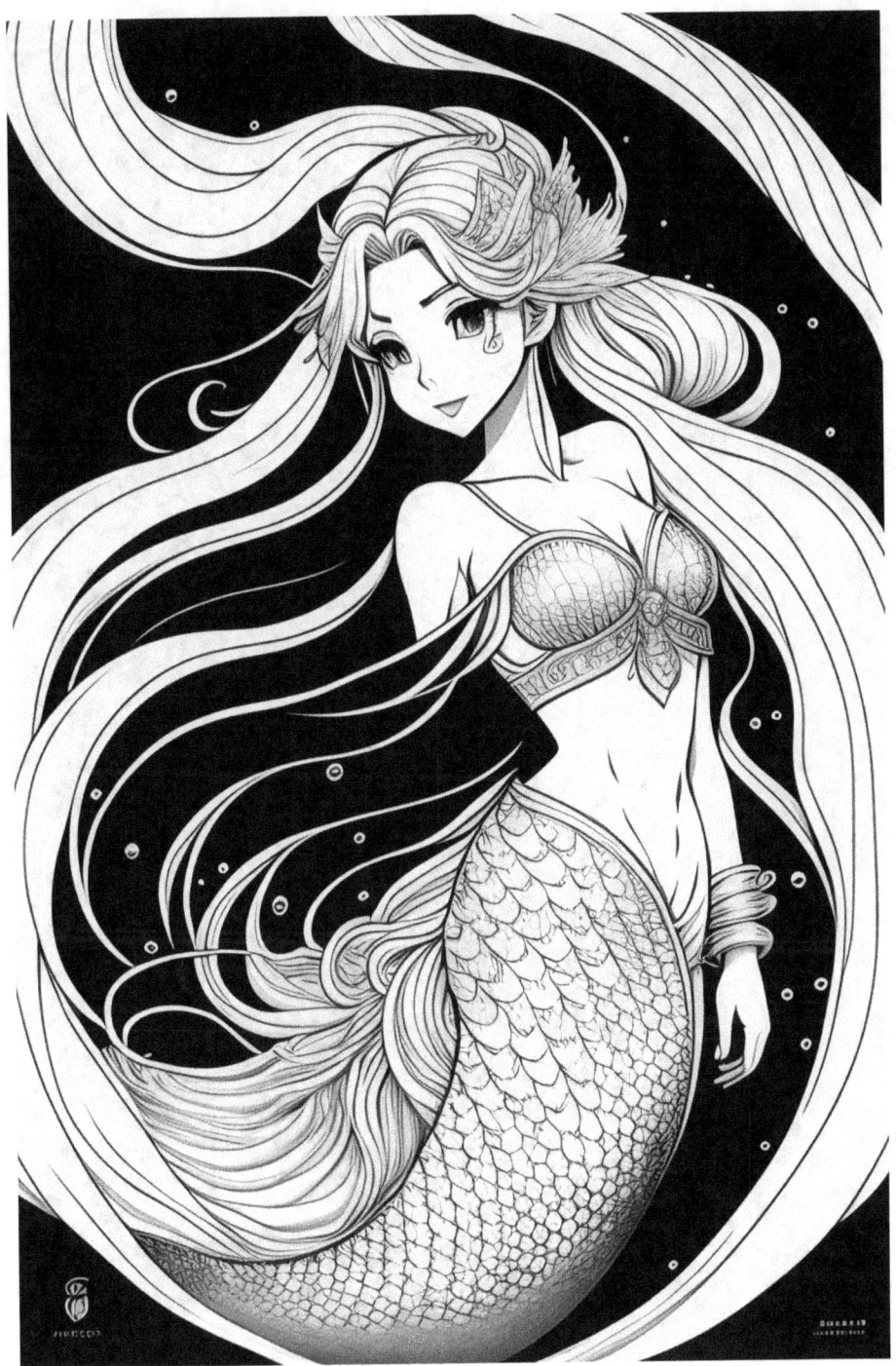

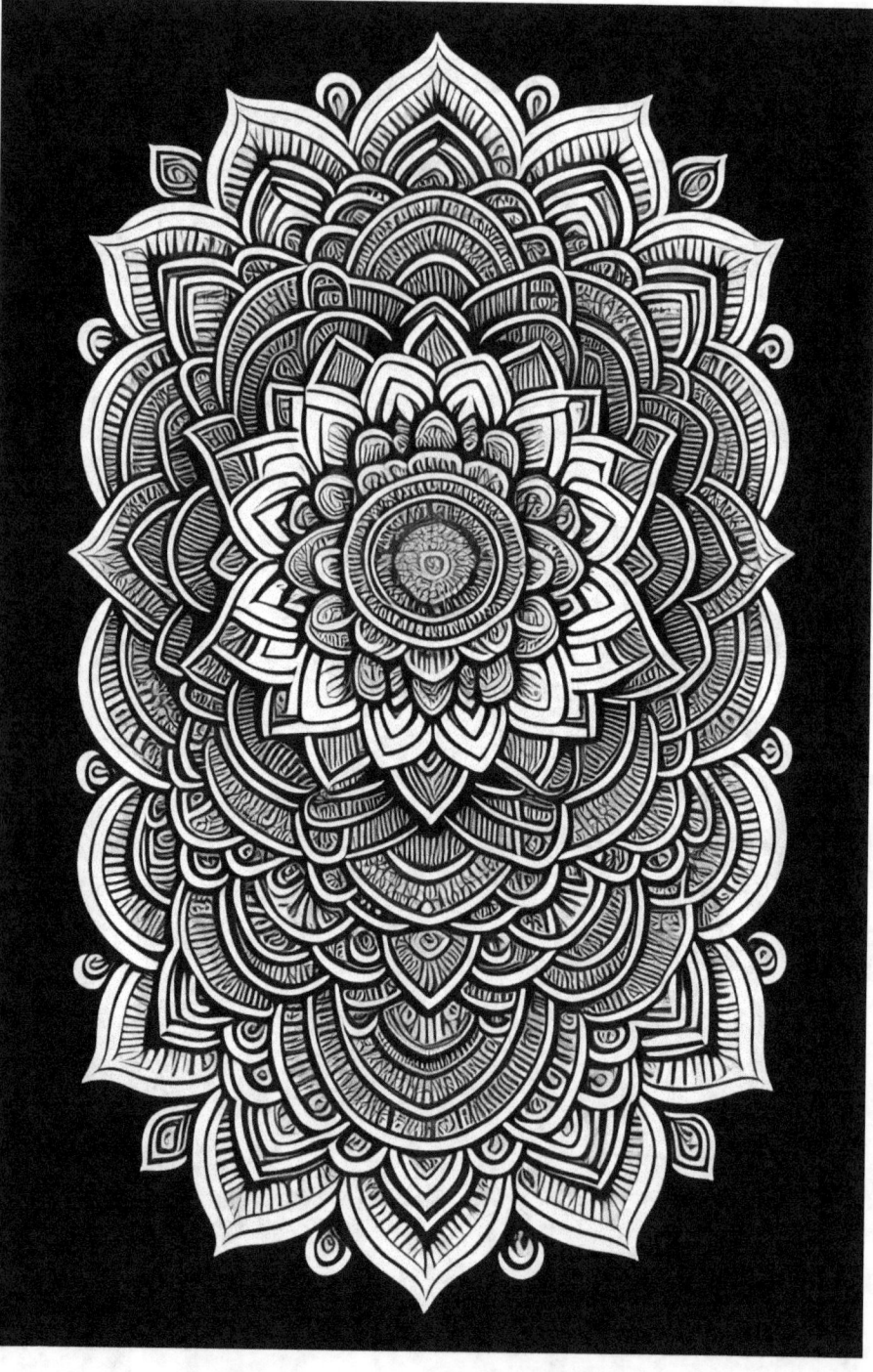

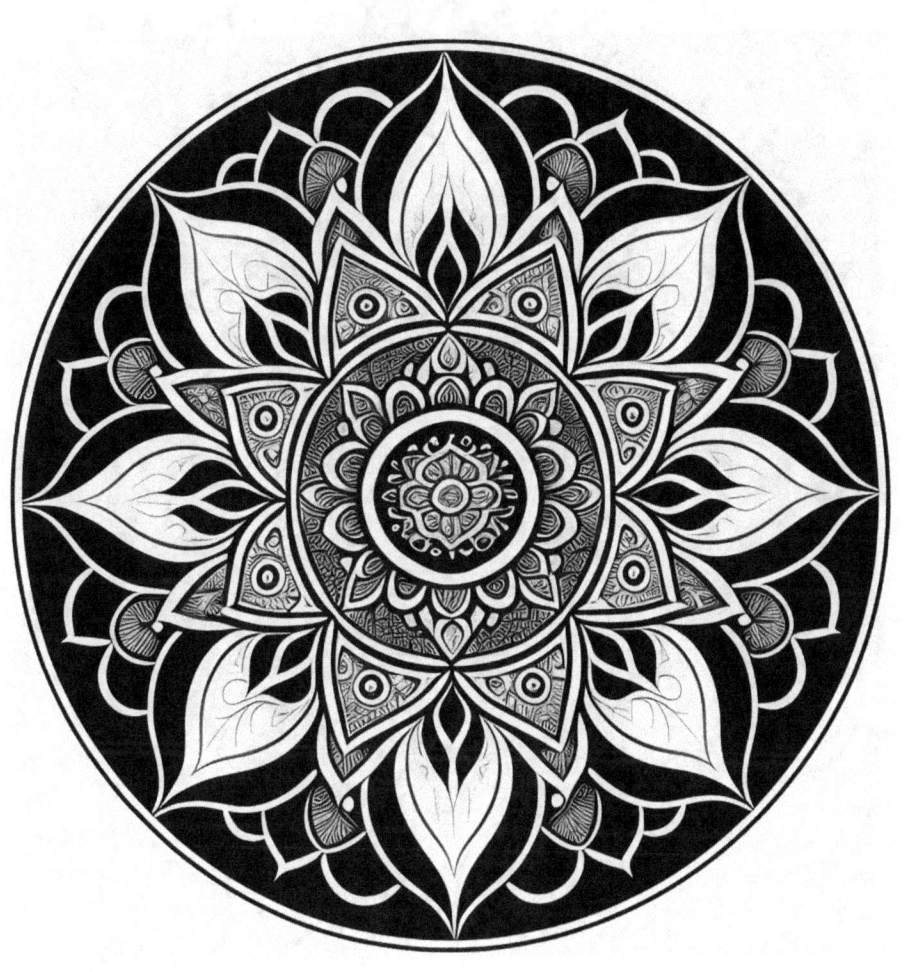

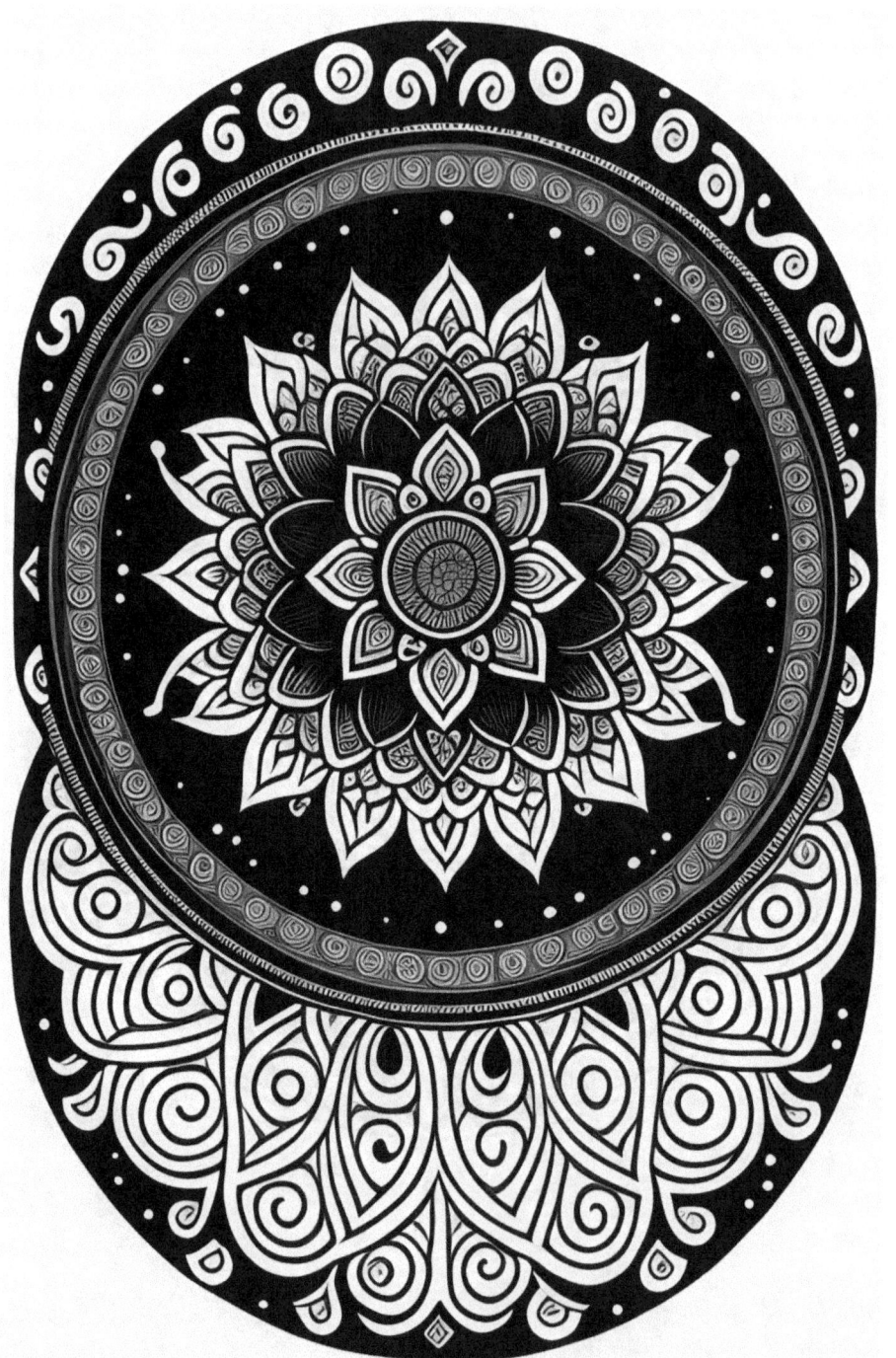

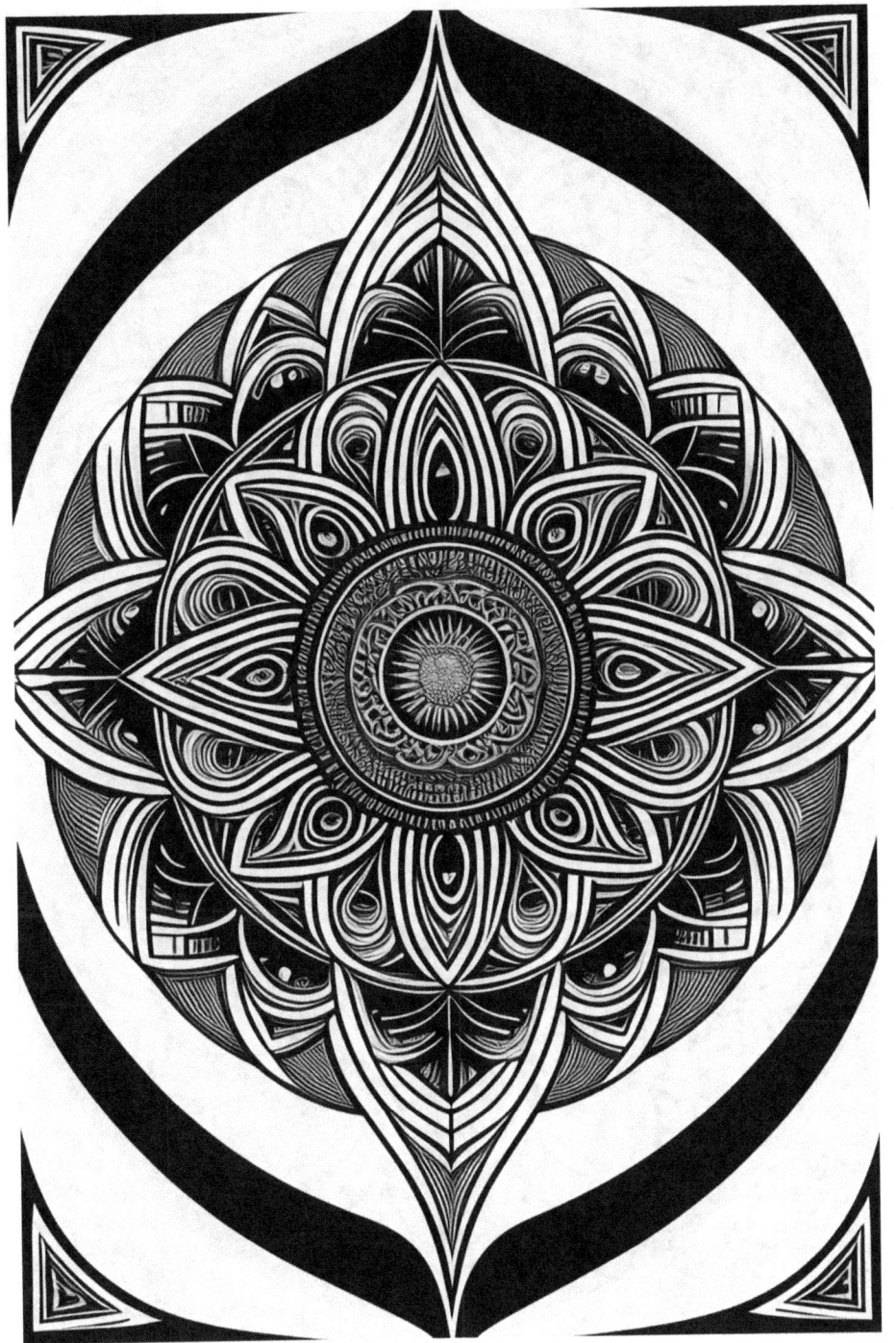

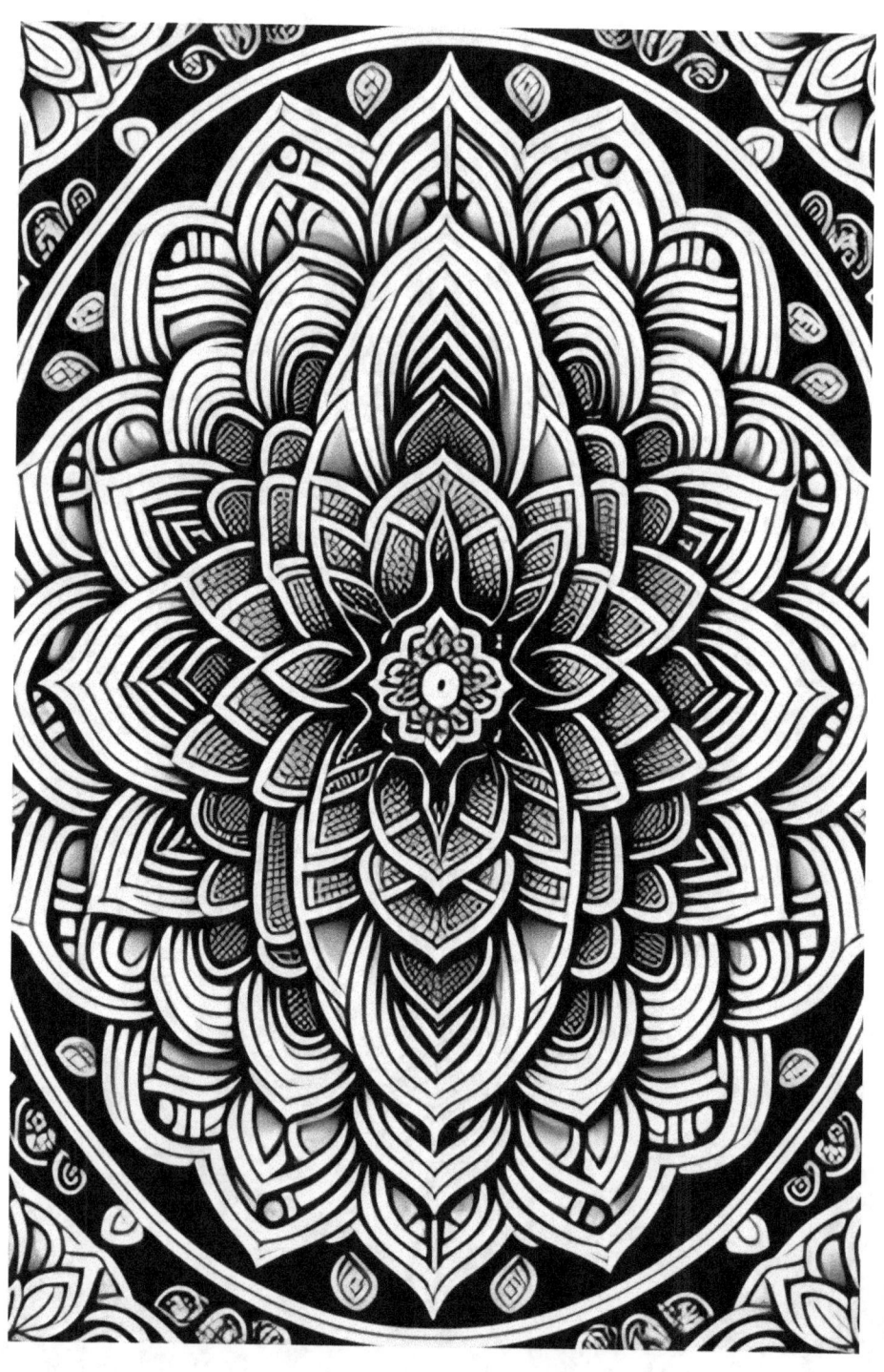

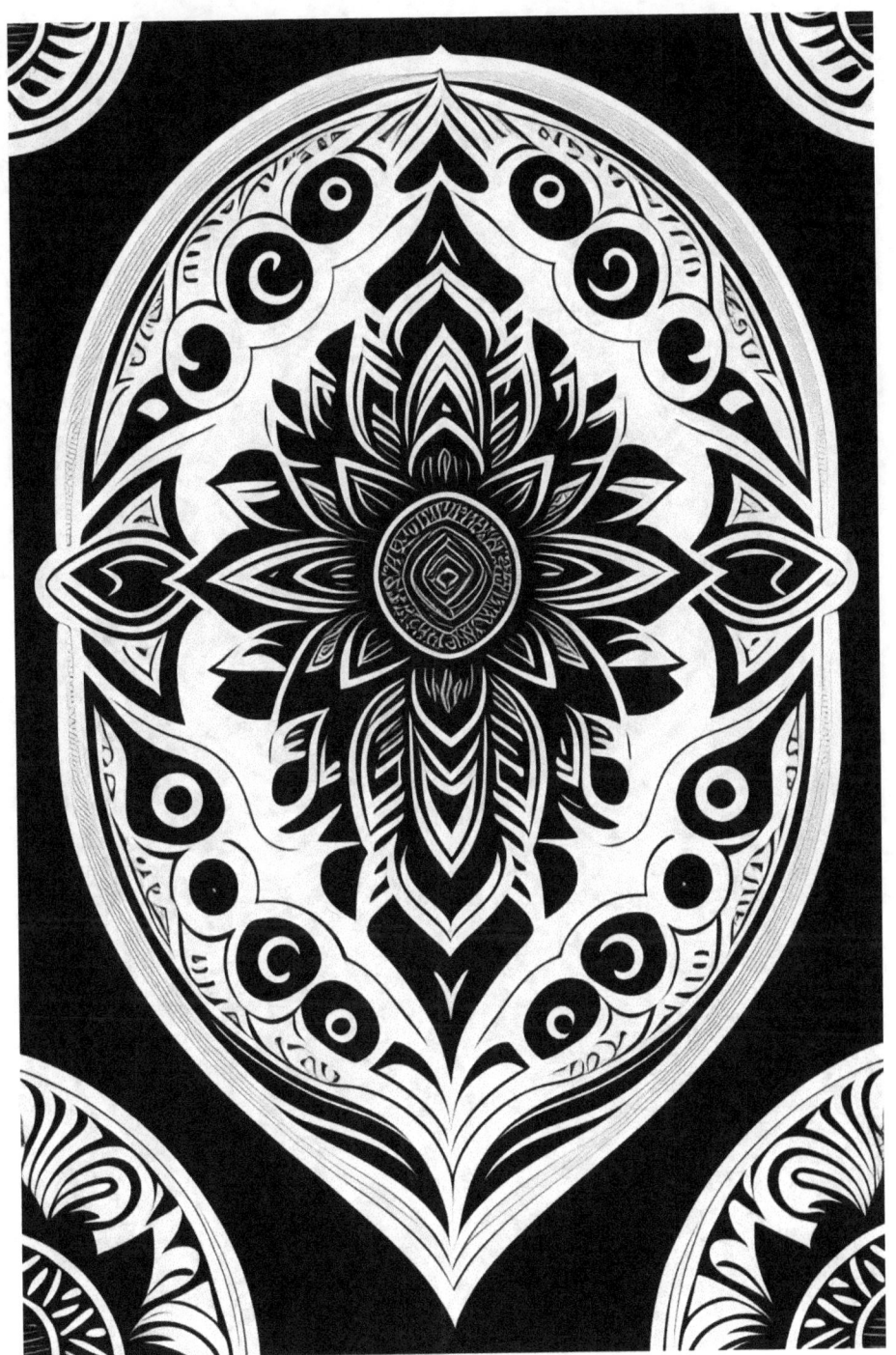

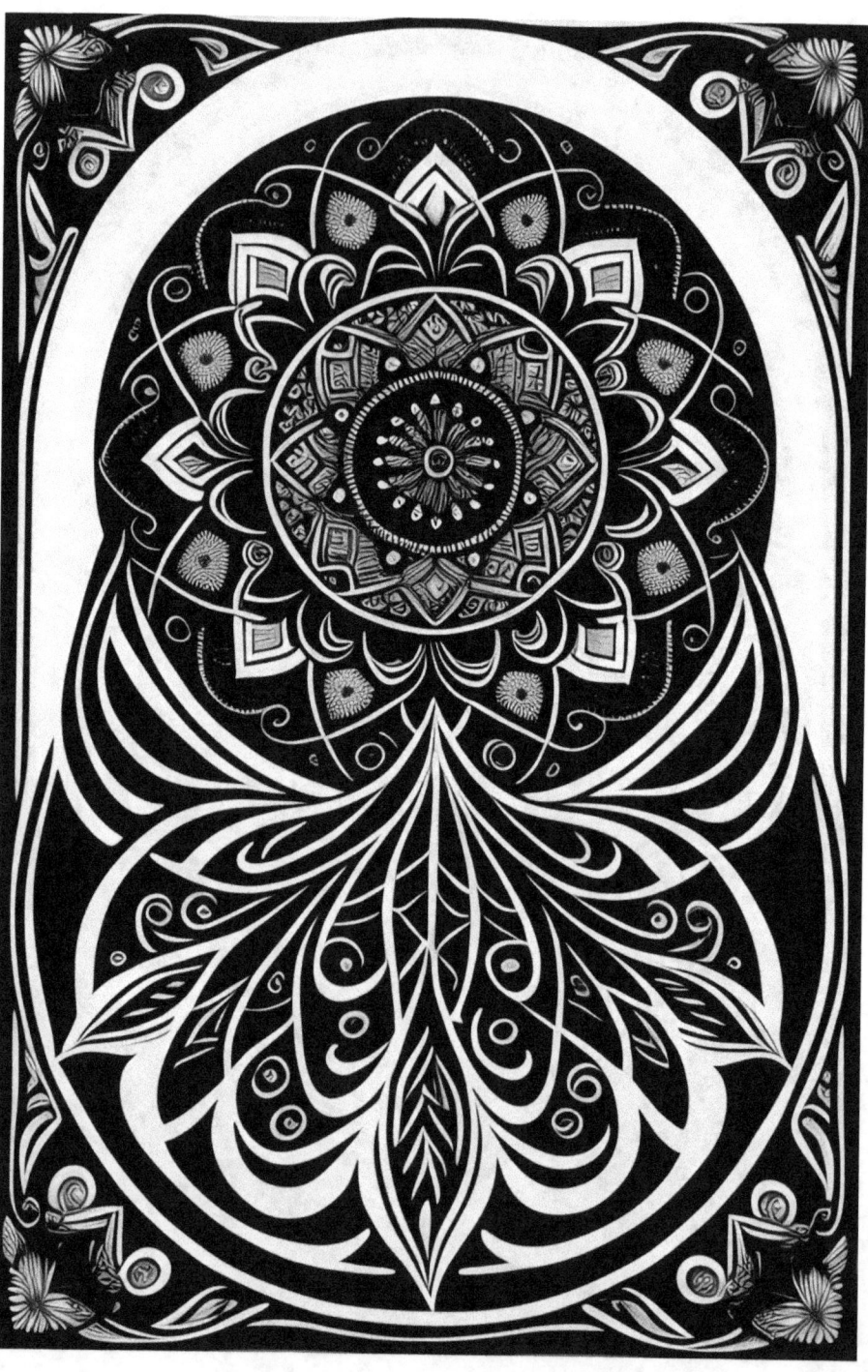

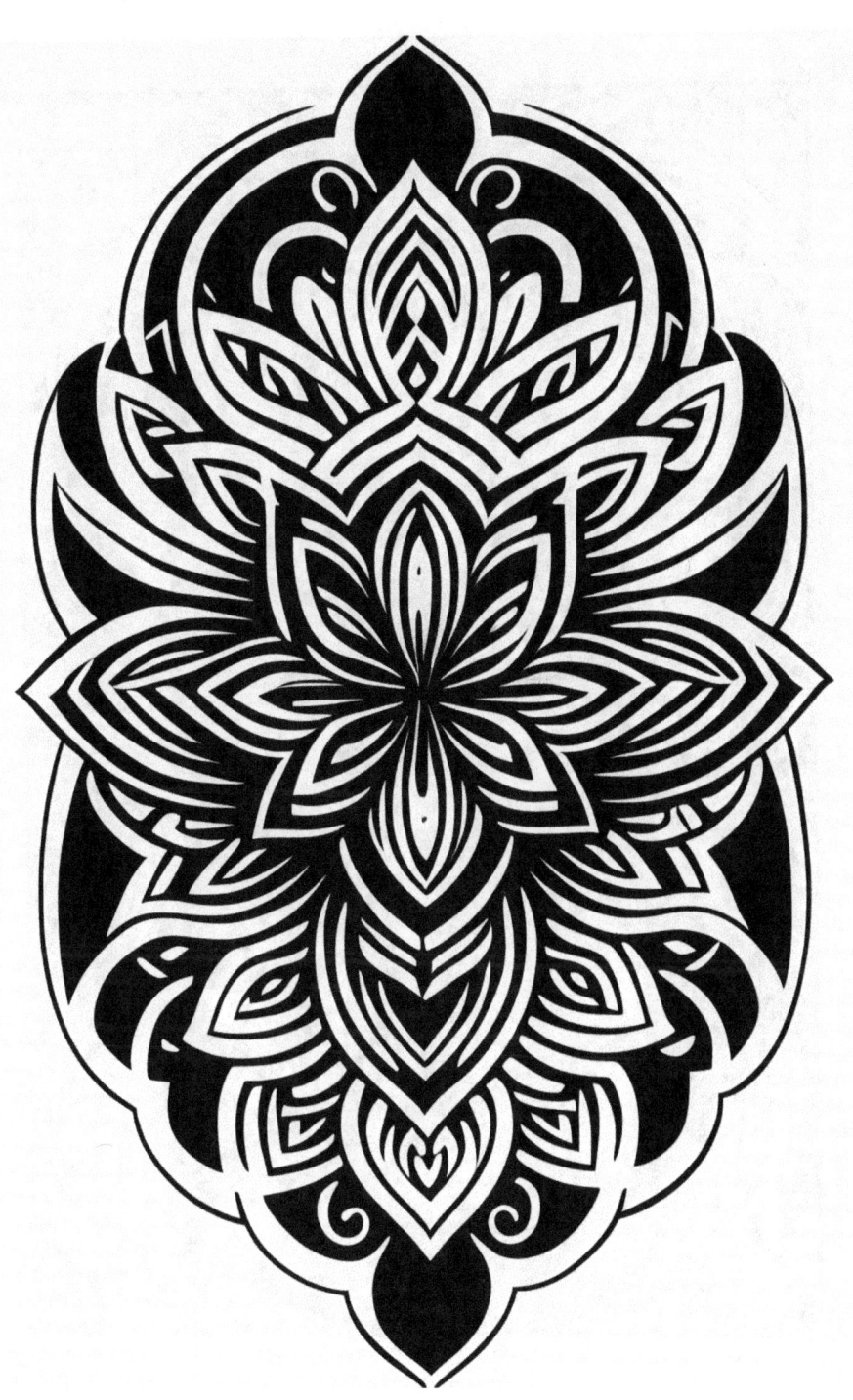

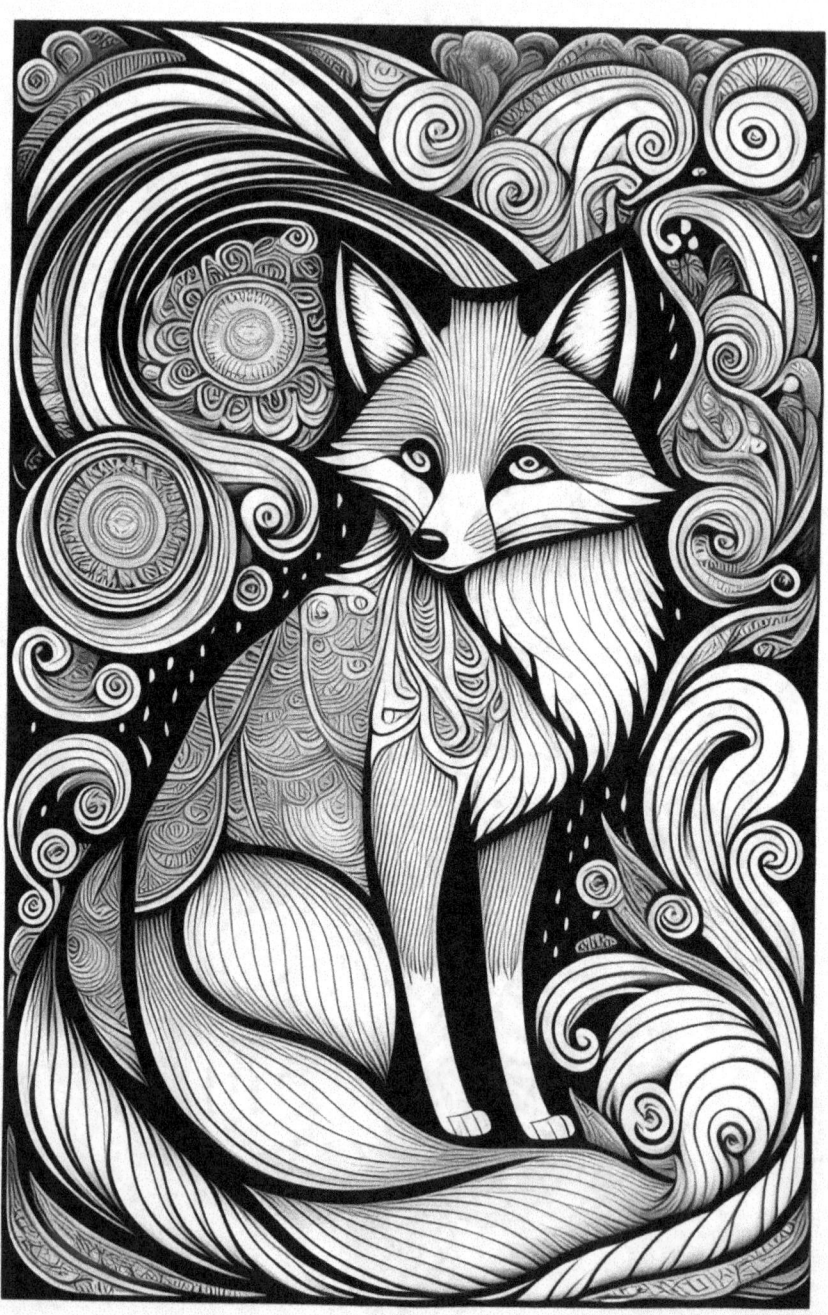

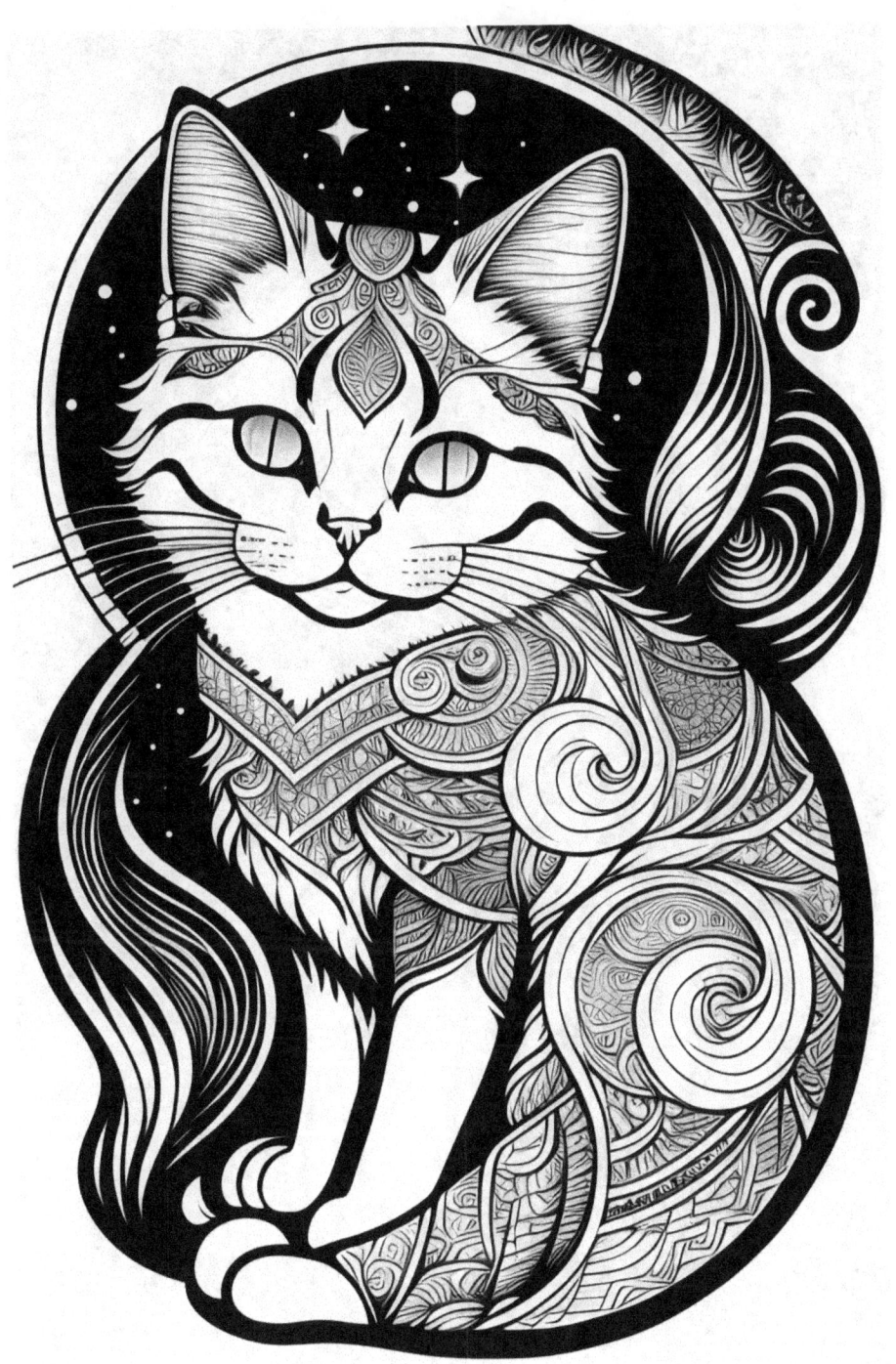

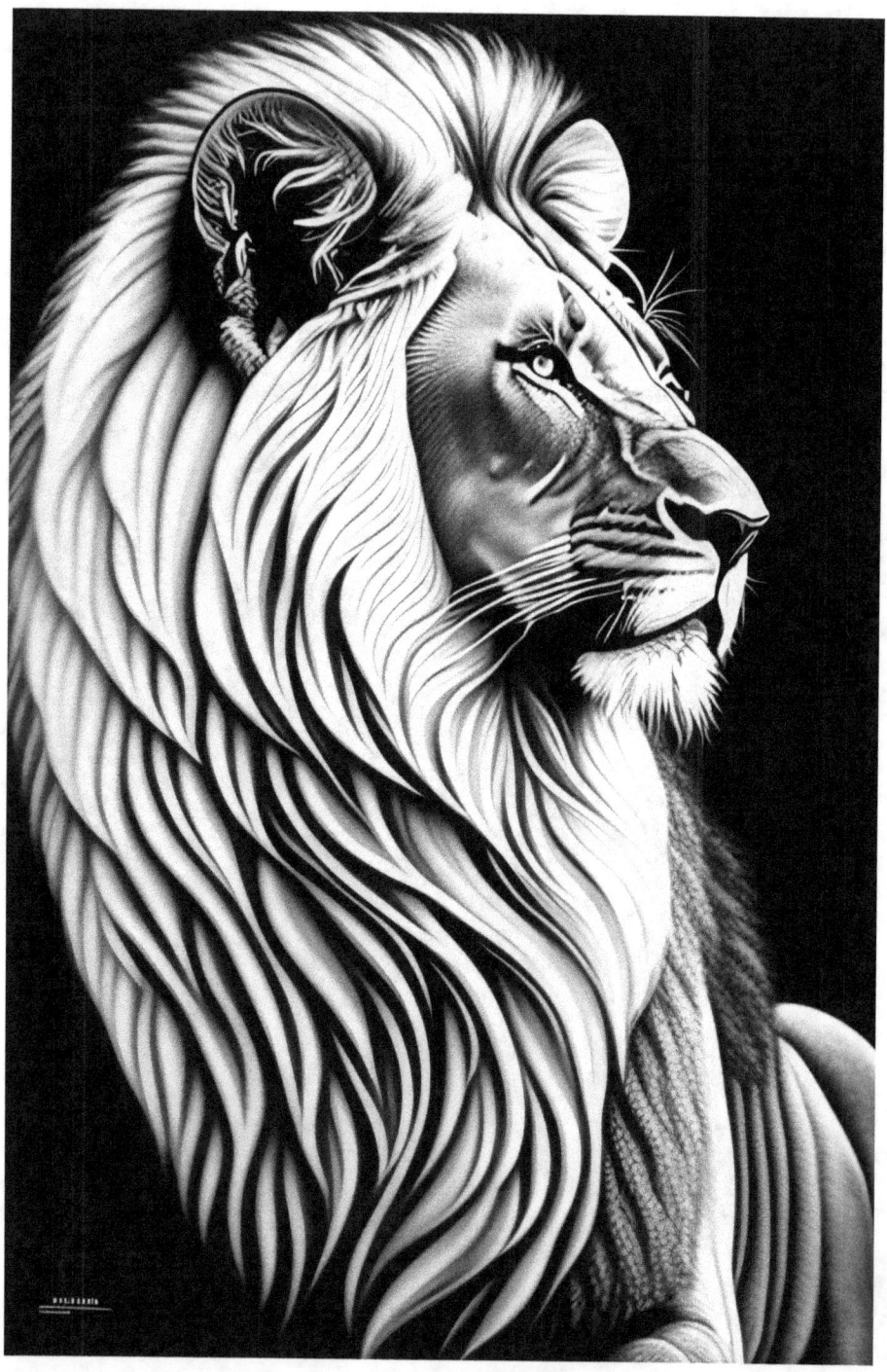

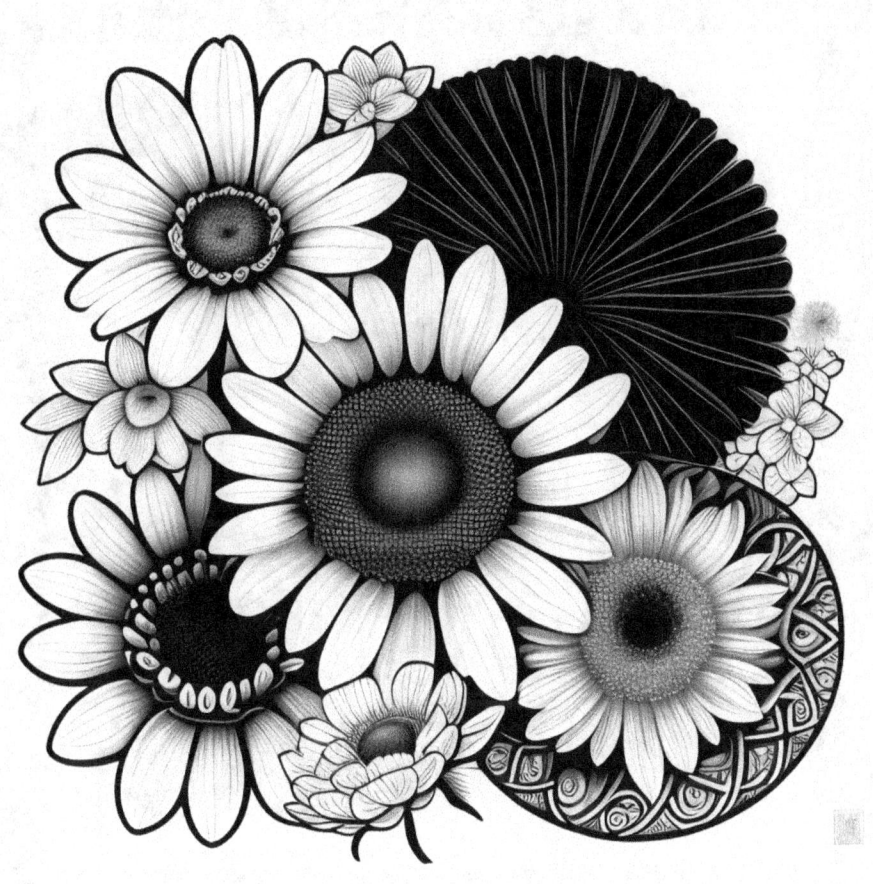

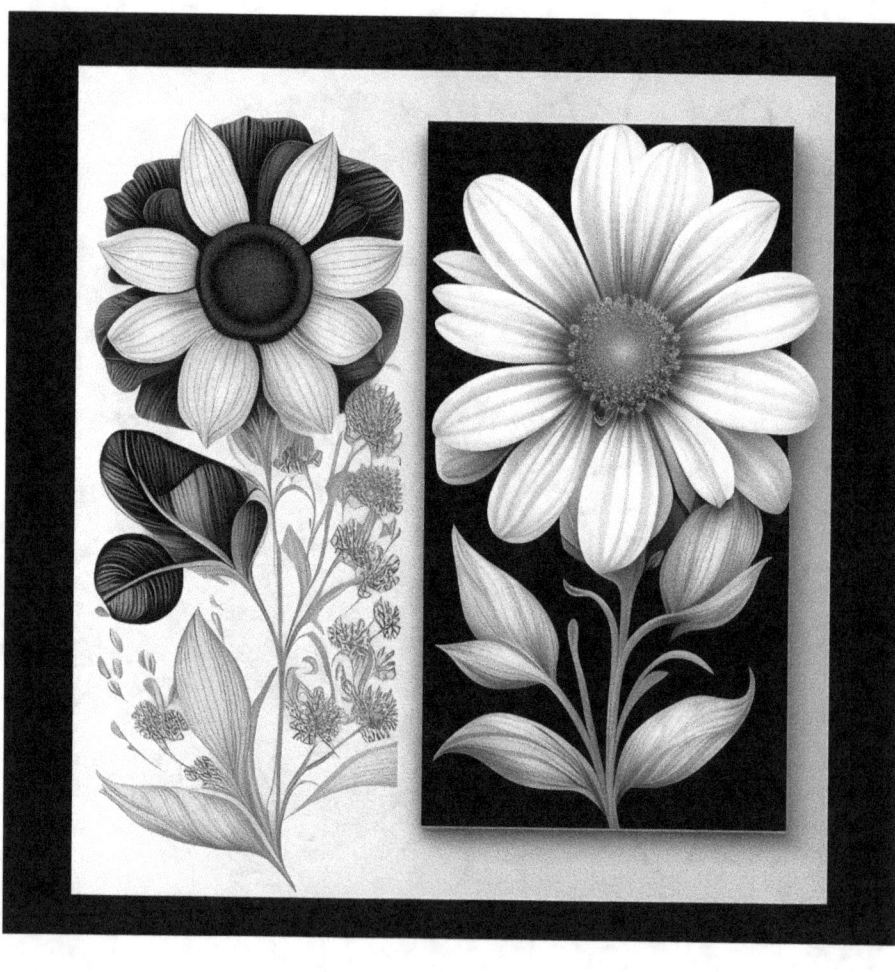

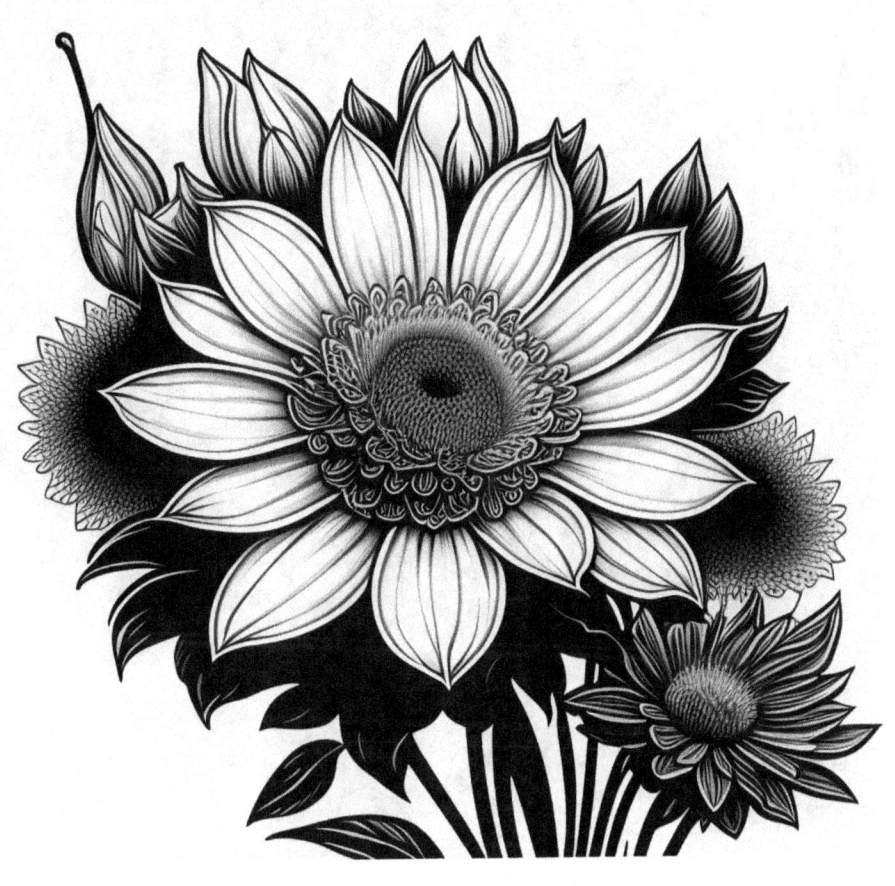

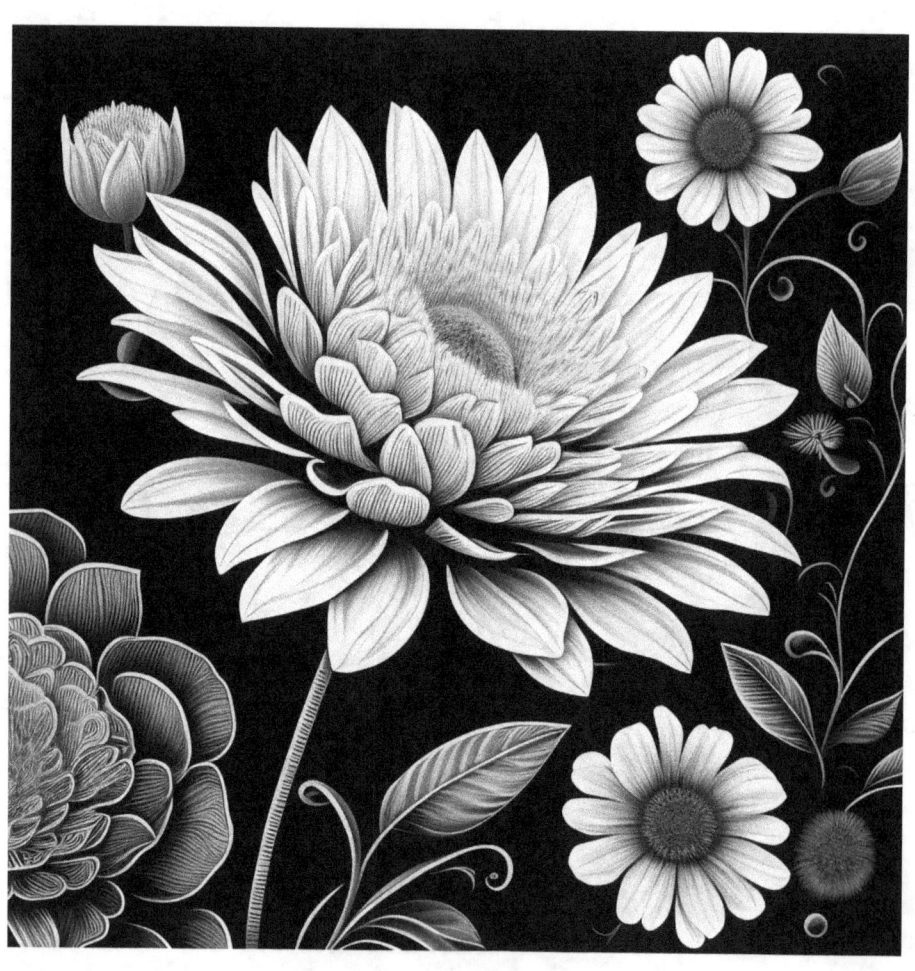

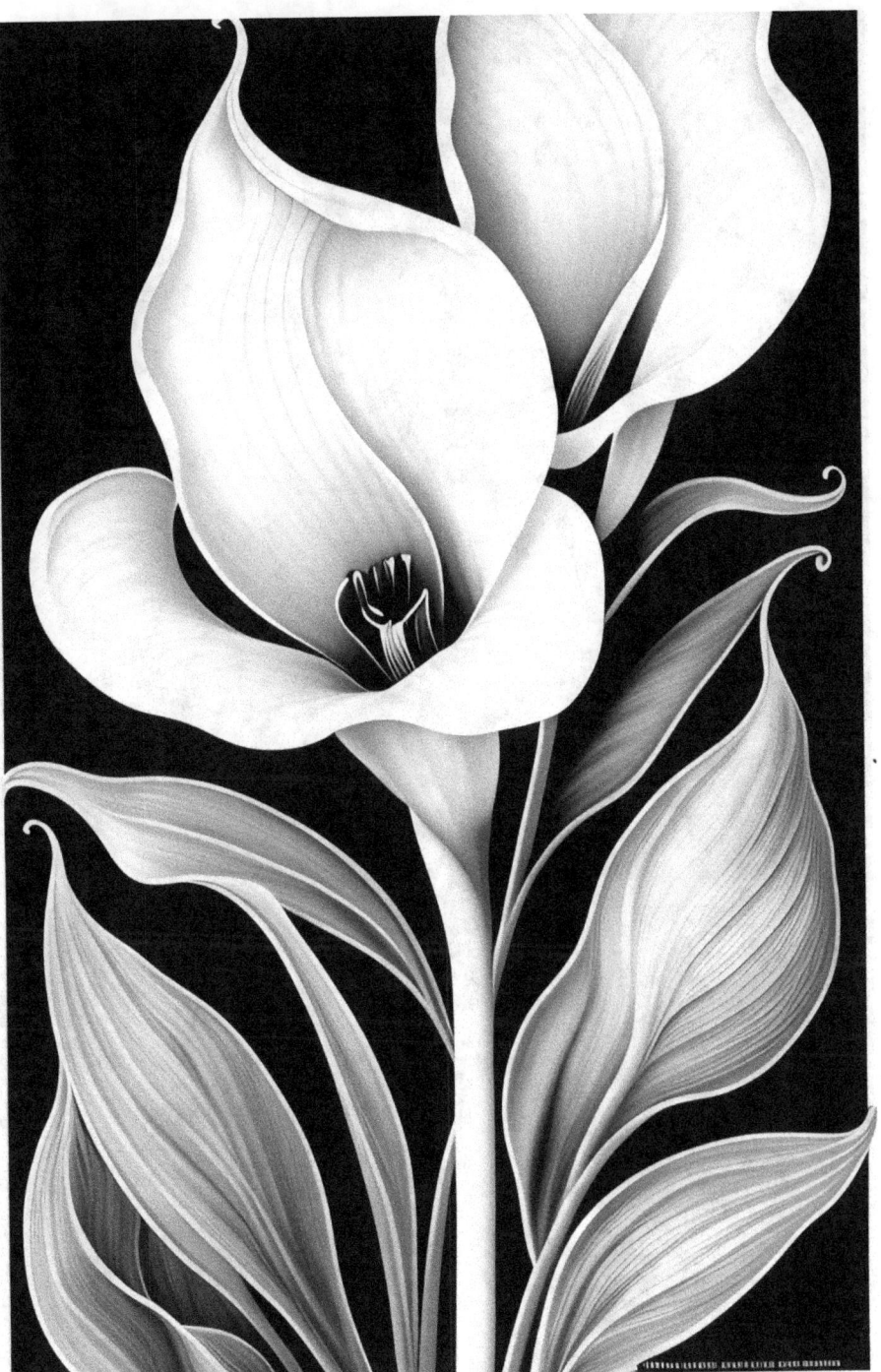

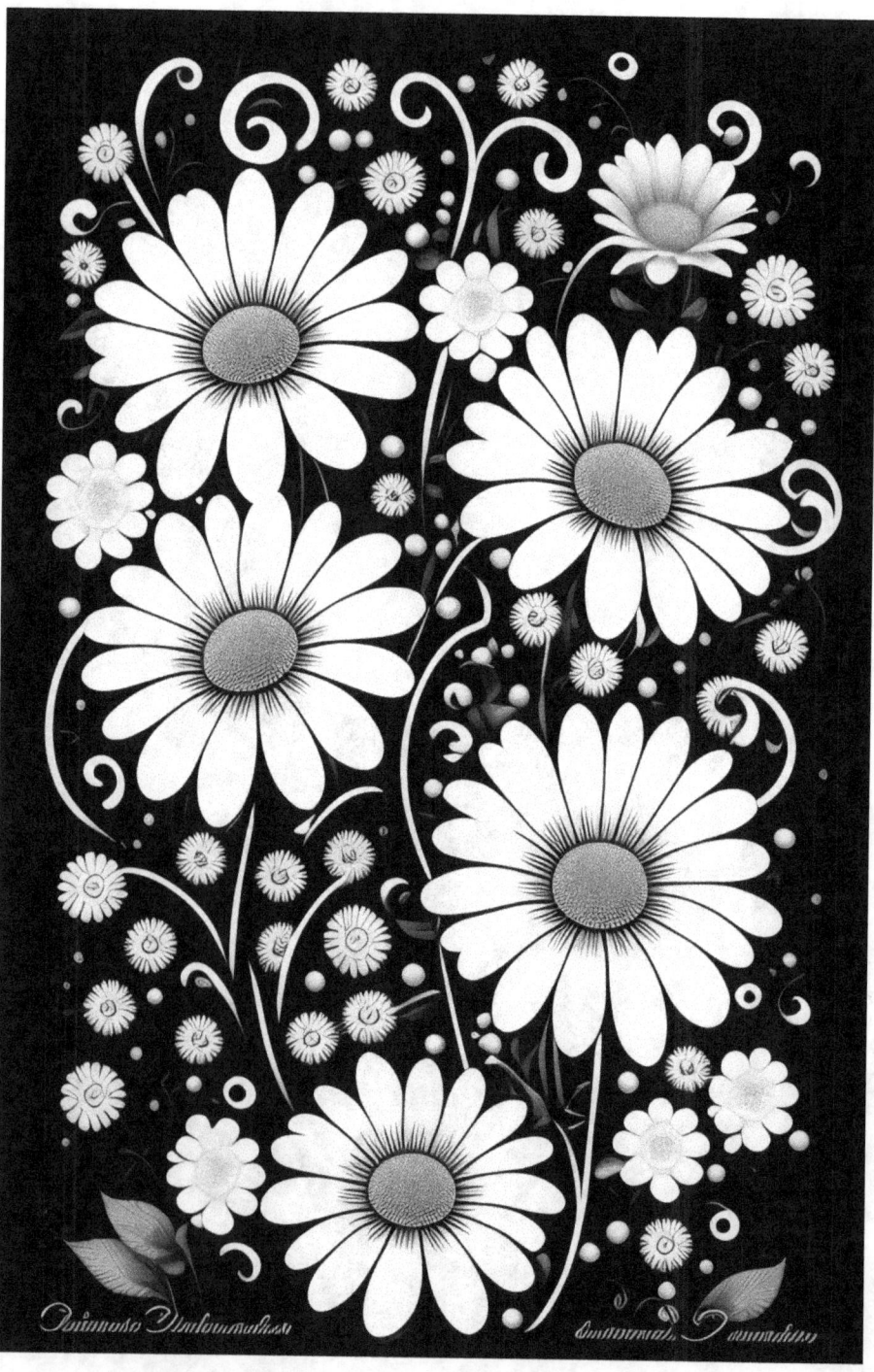

Conclusion

As you reach the end of the "Awesome Coloring Book for Adults," take a moment to reflect on the journey you've embarked upon. Through the act of coloring, you've unleashed your creativity, found moments of peace, and allowed your imagination to soar.

Each stroke of color has been a form of self-expression, a way to connect with your inner artist. As you close the book, remember that the experience doesn't have to end here.

Carry the lessons learned – the importance of self-care, the power of creativity, and the beauty of embracing stillness – into your daily life.

Let the inspiration you've found within these pages guide you to new artistic endeavors and moments of tranquility.

May this book continue to be a source of joy and relaxation, reminding you of the endless possibilities that lie within your own imagination.

Keep coloring, keep creating, and keep nurturing your creative spirit.

www.ingramcontent.com/pod-product-compliance
Lightning Source LLC
Chambersburg PA
CBHW070424240526
45472CB00020B/1194